Why You are Acting that Way in your Love Relationship

(A Love Psychology Book)

For Single and Married

N. Stephen

N. Stephen

Why you are acting that way in your
Love-Relationship

Formatted and Published By:
Space-Era Data Service of Work-Data Group
www.onlineworkdata.com,
www.onlineworkdata.org

First Edition

(©) 2013 N. Stephen

ISBN-13: 978-1483986357
ISBN-10: 1483986357

Word of Knowledge

"The question of love is one that cannot be evaded. Whether or not you claim to be interested in it, from the moment you are alive you are bound to be concerned with love, because love is not just something that happens to you: it is a certain special way of being alive. Love is, in fact, an intensification of life, a completeness, a fullness, a wholeness of life."

(Thomas Merton)

Dedication

This book is dedicated to my Mum, Mrs. N. Grace, and Miss Onyinyechi Udo Chijioke, but its revelational knowledge is of God's gift, therefore all the glory is to Him.

Contents

Acknowledgment

I must credit the authors of two great books, which I read before the development of this book. *"The Power of Subconscious mind;* written by Harry W. Carpenter," and *"Think and Grow Rich (a black-choice);* written by Dennis Kimbro and Napoleon Hill". The former helped me in the logical analysis over the nature of love, and love relationship. Beside, issues like the subconscious and conscious mind were borrowed from it. The latter inspired me to bring the 'thought' into a book. My gratitude goes to these authors.

I must acknowledge Helen Fisher for her great concept concerning the three stages of love, and Alexander Moseley for his good article concerning the Western Philosophy of Love.

Finally is Mr. George Urim for his frantic effort to make sure every page of this book is touched for grammatical corrections, and Miss Beloved Osi who helped for the review and correction of words.

Preface

For over million years and until these present days in the act of thought driven, many people have questioned their minds over the nature and existence of love, and love relationship. In the provisions of answers, different forms of ideologies and philosophies have been developed from time to time. To join the wagon train, I wrote this book, which is to serve both single and married persons.

Why You Are Acting That Way in Your Love Relationship is a book that derived a new philosophy, and expressed the pyschological state of love, the nature, and existence of love relationship in a different view.

For you as a being, it exposes the two strong factors responsible for your temperament (i.e. quality of mind) over the way you behave, reciprocate and response in your love life and relationship. These two strong factors are in one hand *"the state of your conscious and subconscious mind"* and in the other hand, a popular economic concept called *'marginal utility'*.

Although, it all began like a thought, and had agitated on my mind for over 10 years. During these years, I have researched, had diversified thoughts, and reflected on the issues with different categories of people for that long, then drew conclusions with proven knowledge. The achieved knowledg is original as the book reveals new knowledge to humanity.

As for background, I am a social scientist, economist, and habitually a 'natural thinker' who often thinks about those natural phenomena that govern man's way of life, in a manner of reasonning, knowledge, behaviour, value, and belief system.

However, if you are reading this book, mind you that its content is of different fields of learning. These include that of sociology, psychology, religion, economics, philosophy, biology, et cetera.

Besides, the things you must put aside in order to gain the expected knowledge impact are *conformity, sentiment,* and *bias,* for they were not in consideration when I did the work. In this life, conformity, sentiment, and bias have significant roles in our thought conclusions, and behavioural patterns. Take for instance, in the case of conformity, all of us are conforming in hundred of ways. However, the ability of not conforming both in learning, reasoning, value, and belief system is better. Therefore, it is better if you find your own way of understanding the nature of love, and by doing so; it will help you properly manage your love life as a single or married person. In addition, it will also save you from psychoactive tendency, lovelorn, lovesick, and heartbreak.

N. Stephen,
August 2013

The Birth of this Book

The birth of this book is not by accident. There are ideas, questions, concepts, experiences, and conditions that formed together for its development, and this was not a day, neither a month, nor a year work, but was of 10 years of time.

My love relationship experiences, questioning mind approach, the course (economics) I studied, personal interaction with people, online and offline articles and books that I read, all were concocted in given birth of this book within the period.

How does the development of the book begin? It began like a thought around April 2003 when I asked myself a question over the 'meaning of love' and the *forces* behind most of our uncontrollable response in love relationship. From 2003 to 2008, it existed as thought on my mind, but, before 2008, within 2007, I conducted an interview with 30 persons regarding to the issues and engaged them in discussion concerning it, and then read many articles and books in order to support the outcome of the interview.

In 2009, I wrote the first manuscript, and continue with other findings, which lasted until the day the book was finally writen in the year 2013.

What really encouraged me was the year 2012 publication of my first book titled: *Applied Microsoft Excel (App-XL) in Statistics, Economics, Business, and Finance Perspective: For Microsoft Excel Users and Beginners*. It was published and sales by CreateSpace LLC of USA, an Amazon.Com Company.

Nevertheless, since the book is of psychological in kind, and as been mentioned in the preface, its popular parlance is of different field of learning, which includes that of sociology, religion, economics, philosophy, biology, et cetera.

Disclaimer

The purpose of this book is to reveal the forces behind your love relationship, and as well let you know *why you are acting that way in your love relationship and life*. It is a counseling book for love relationship, and a guide to build and manage ones love life and relationship. It is expressively on the notion of *"whys, answers,* and *reasons"*, and it may expose your love relationship strengths and weaknesses.

Although, you may have been on the tolerance, cheating, or unfavourable side of your marriage or affair, the result in this book is challenging, practical, clearly written, and very workable for certain solutions. To some extent, one can also use it to create a self worth, rebuild a brokenhearted, and create personal happiness. But, to seek a redress through an attitudinal and behavioural change because of what you learnt from it, may bring misunderstanding in your marriage, or relationship, perhaps due to the kind of partner you have, so mind your approach for the author is not responsible. Moreover, if you are indecision characterised person, mind you that this book will not force you to change, since positive behavioural change comes only through self-discipline or concious control over lifestyle. For sometimes, we failed, not because we lack the proper knowledge, but due to inadequate behavioural response. Therefore, the way forward depends on self-discipline and control, formal training, and ensuring of a proper behavioural pattern. Personally, I suggest that you see a psychologist or pray when issues are beyond your control.

Prologue

Since the dawn of man, there has been an existence of love relationship, between two the same sex, or two opposite sex. Why everyone feels relationship? Perhaps, it is a concept imprinted in our heart since childhood via experiences, or something we naturally predisposed to do for the need of someone to care for us. Moreover, for whatever reason, it (relationship) is important, therefore needed like food, water, and oxygen.

We all need it; this is because everyone wants someone on his or her side. For instance, when we are in a relationship, we feel incredible, happy, and being possess by a deep sense of appreciation. In addition, get our strengths and weaknesses improved by expecting our partner to dictate, and help us make corrections, thus get the best in us, increases our sense of welbeing and, most cases gain the benefit of lowering stress and blood pressure in our biological system with the aim of increasing our health and longevity.

Of negative course of action, people commit sucide, murder, hate each other, dropout of schools, and act lunatically just to feel or remain in relationship.

One may ask, what forces does a relationship possess in order to influence our lives so much? It is attached with a driving force known as *compounded-feeling*, which runs in our entire body, and it is been powered by emotion. It is invisible, and to a large extends difficult to be control. This is because it exists in the subconscious mind, and that is why, it makes us reasonable and stupid most times.

Although, it is difficult to be control, but we can play it with caution. This depends during its formation by outlining the boundaries cum principles, which will guide us. Yes, with boundries cum principles, and as well much carefulness, we can be on the winning-side, and not always on the receiving-end, meaning that our heart may be fill with joy or bitterness, but all depend on our adopted approach.

Nevertheless, as we stated in the 'preface', the key aim of this book is to expose the two factors that are responsible for the way we behave in our love life, and relationship. Beside, there are inferences over which these two factors have been proved to be true, take for instance of this story;

> *I have been a mediator in many broken love relationship and this particular case added more questions to my thought. Placing over my desktop screen around 17.00 GMT on 17TH of Friday, September 2010 is a mail sent to me by Miss Evelyn Jackson. Back in 2007, I helped Miss Jackson secured admission with University of Glasgow that was during my working time with Admission-Place Services, which were rendering educational services to international students.*

> *Then, later she introduced her friend Samuel Brain to me; all this was still in 2007, as I became an intimate friend to them.*

> *On August 27, 2010, suprisingly, I met her in Yahoo Messenger chat room. We exchanged cell phone numbers, and she offered me calls frequently. However, in one of our conversations, she asked, "Steve how is she? Are you still going out with her? I knew she is referring to circumstance, which I told her then, but I replied, "No, she failed with time, and I gave up the pursuit". Imagining what could possible happened; She slumped in dejection and asked an open question "God why? Why is it that in most occasions when you love some one, in a reverse, the person will not love you? Steve, I am tired of Brain too". She continued, "do you know that there is nothing a woman can do in showing love to a man, I have not done to him, yet, I cannot explain his problem. I know what he passed through before he got me. When we started new, he was so nice and lovely until I surrendered all to him. However, today, I am solely the pillar of our relationship while he is indifferent. The entirely issue is I am confused and can't really say why I'm engulfed in the whole thing".*

By the power of imagination, I saw a face with a cry of despair, so at this point; I collected Brain phone number from her and had a telephone chat with him. It was a nice conversation, he sounds so innocent and truly he has newer been cheating on her, but cannot explain why been occasionally indifferent. He said, "She is always there for me, but I don't know why I am no longer caring much about her. The whole thing started since she made herself so available to me". "On the situation, what is your thought over the whole issue?" I asked. "She threatened to quit the relationship and I won't let her. I need her and my heart is yelling for her, Steve help me, I don't think I will let her go." He continues, "She is the source of my happiness, do you know I have loss energy to do most things, and I can't concentrate with my work" as he concluded.

The whole experience gave me different thoughts over what might be the cog in the wheel of progress. Relating their circumstances to the psychological and satisfaction side of human behaviour, I made some significant conclusions.

In the case of Evelyn's behaviour:

- She added much labour of love and got lovelorn as a reward,
- She made herself so available (abundantly), thus, became too cheap,
- She never gives Brain a chance to think about her, so he lost feeling for her because thought creates feeling,
- She failed to play seasonal indifferent game. (A game where you behaved as if you do not fancy your relationship),
- She has created many good pictures of the relationship on her subconscious mind, thus, lacks the willpower to question the ugly-side of the relationship as her subconscious mind often overpower the conscious side of her mind in decision-making concerning the relationship.

However, in the case of Brain:

- He was suffocated from Evelyn's always-available attitude, so the desire was killed, thus the satisfaction seens to be no longer there,
- He is fully convinced that she loves him, so he began to give her less attention,
- The recent panic on his side is because she is threatening to quit the relationship.

From the foregoing story, we all are familiar with such circumstance, even in blood relationship, man and woman relationship, courtship or marriage, experience shows there are always circumstances to ask the following questions:

- What is love? Is it real or ideal?
- Is there any correlation between romantic relationship and human productivity?
- Can we differentiate infatuation from love?
- Is true love attainable?
- What are the causes of lovesick or lovelorn?
- Like many people believe, a man loves once in life time", is that true?
- Is there anyway, we can protect our mind in love relationship?
- Can I be in control of my relationship?
- What is my personality type, in love relationship?
- How do I know the reasons why someone accepted me for a relationship?
- What is behind my unstableness in relationship decision making?
- I do everything to make him/her happy, yet he never likes them, why?
- Why do people I love, do not return the same to me?
- Why in most relationship, we fight for dominance, and
- Others not mentioned.

Generally, how can one feel true love, expecially when we consider the propensity rate of peoples' doubt over the reality of true love? For instance, millions of people are in lovelorn or lovesick, many heart have been broken, there are many broken marriages, millions of jittery and jilted lovers, predators and others have caused many people failure in academic, business, suicide, loss of energy, poor attitude to work, lack of focus, no rest of mind, and other illnesses.

The issues are of contemporary and by taking a ride with this book, being unbias and rationale in mind; one can answer the above-stated questions.

The three key terms of this book

For better understanding, we must differentiate these terms, *particularity, personality,* and *trait,* and as well must not forget their meaning because of their frequency used in this book.

Particularity: It is the condition of personal individuality to an individual person. In other words, it is the condition of being peculiar to an individual person rather than a group of persons.

Personality: It is person's set of character. In other words, it is the totality of somebody's attitudes, interests, behavioural patterns, emotional responses, social roles, and other individual traits that endure over long a period.

Trait: It is a single character of personality that distinquishes a person from others.

Chapter One

THE PHILOSOPHY OF LOVE

Introduction

N othing drives the World like the forces of love. It is the most pressing need of everyone, both singles and couples want to love, and be loved. For the greatest commandment of God is for us to love Him, and then love ourselves. Align to this purpose, Poets, Authors, and Scientists are in works to bring better understanding concerning the reality of love[1]. Although, in the past, it was not so, when Scientists refused to involve in the study. But, during the past decades, in a broad range of disciplines, they have had a change of heart about love, and as well participate in the study[2]. However, the philosophy behind love has been in contention among these Authors, Poets, and Scientists. This is the reason why there are many philosophical treatment of love in many sub-disciplines, and therefore the main purpose of this chapter.

---

1. Bonny Albo of About.Com Guide (www.dating.about.com/od/intimacy/qt/whatislove.htm)
2. Paul Gray, Hannah Bloch, and Sally Donnelly of Time Inc., 2011, (www.time.com/time/magazine/article/0,9171,97763,00.html)

As Alexander Moseley observed[3];

> *The philosophical treatment of love transcends a variety of sub-disciplines including epistemology, metaphysics, religion, human nature, politics and ethics. Often statements or arguments concerning love, its nature, and role in human life for example, connect to one or all the central theories of philosophy and is often compared with or examined in the context of the philosophies of sex and gender. The task of a philosophy of love is to present the appropriate issues in a cogent manner, drawing on the relevant theories of human nature desire, ethics and so on.*

However, the aim here is to examine love in the context of Western philosophies, and a layman view, and make a conclusion.

In the Western philosophies, It was seen better to address them in quote, which was done.

The content featured the work of Alexander Moseley in his reviewed of other philosophers' works. Moreover, for the layman view, the statement is on the meaning of love and form of love. The result gotten from a sample questionnaire was presented, and finally, comes a deductive conclusion from all the sample works.

Expectation

At the end of this chapter, the expectation is that you should be able to establish a belief or philosophy concerning the way love, its nature and role touches your life. You are as well to know the exact philosophy of love that has been ruling your love life and relationship. In this condition, your ability to construct or principled your own philosophy of love and identifying the role of love in your life is also an expected gain.

Why developing one's philosophy

Personal beliefs and philosophies are good. Man is dialectic to his environment, thus the prevailing philosophy or belief accepted by him has a large role in his way of life, including social relationship and love life. In love life, many are living with too much unsolved questions hovering over their minds. For instance, the nature of love, love-relationship, happiness and love, health and love, et cetera.

---

3. Alexander Moseley observation is culled from; www.classical-formations.com. Mind you, that website contents are bound for updating, sorry if the information is removed or updated from its present place.

The Western Philosophies of Love

It is conventional in Western Philosophies that love has a nature, but some have argued against it. For an examination and reviewing of such arguments, we look into the work written by Alexander Moseley of classical foundation[4]:

...in English tradition, the word "love", which is derived from Germanic forms of the Sanskrit lubln (desire) is broadly defined and hence imprecise, which generates first order problems of definition and meaning that are resolved to some extent by the reference to the Greek terms, Eros, Philia, and Agape.

Eros

The term eros (Greek erasthai) is used to refer to that part of love constituting a passionate, intense desire for something; it is often referred to as a sexual desire, hence the modern notion of "erotic" (Greek erotikos).

In Plato's writings however, eros is held to be a common desire that seeks transcendental beauty-the particular beauty of an individual reminds us of true beauty that exists in the world of Forms or Ideas (Phaedrus 249E: "he who loves the beautiful is called a lover because he partakes of it." Trans. Jowett).

The Platonic-Socratic position maintains that the love we generate for beauty on this earth can never be truly satisfied until we die; but in the meantime, we should aspire beyond the particular stimulating image in front of us to the contemplation of beauty in itself.

The implication of the Platonic theory of eros is that ideal beauty, which is reflected in the particular images of beauty we find, becomes interchangeable across people and things, ideas, and art: to love is to love the Platonic form of beauty-not a particular individual, but the element they possess of true (Ideal) beauty. Reciprocity is not necessary to Plato's view of love, for the desire is for the object (of Beauty), than for, say, the company of another and shared values and pursuits.

Many in the Platonic vein of philosophy hold that love is an intrinsically higher value than appetitive or physical desire. Physical desire, they note, is held in common with the animal kingdom. Hence, it is of a lower order of reaction and stimulus than a rationally induced love—that is, a love produced by rational discourse and exploration of ideas, which in turn defines the pursuit of Ideal beauty. Accordingly, the physical love of an object, an idea, or a person in itself is not a proper form of love, love being a reflection of that part of the object, idea, or person, that partakes in Ideal beauty.

---

4. The saying over here is attributes to Alexander Moseley, although he may not be the original writer (which I am not sure), but it was extracted from a work he did, captioned; the nature of Love: Eros, Philia, and Agape. You can check it in www.google.ca

Philia

In contrast to the desiring and passionate yearning of eros, philia entails a fondness and appreciation of the other. For the Greeks, the term philia incorporated not just friendship, but also loyalties to family and polis-one's political community, job, or discipline. Philia for another may be motivated, as Aristotle explains in the Nicomachean Ethics, Book VIII, for the agent's sake or for the other's own sake. The motivational distinctions are derived from love for another because the friendship is wholly useful as in the case of business contacts, or because their character and values are pleasing (with the implication that if those attractive habits change, so too does the friendship), or for the other in who they are in themselves, regardless of one's interests in the matter. The English concept of friendship roughly captures Aristotle's notion of philia, as he writes: "things that cause friendship are: doing kindnesses; doing them unasked; and not proclaiming the fact when they are done" (Rhetoric, II. 4, trans. Rhys Roberts).

Aristotle elaborates on the kinds of things we seek in proper friendship, suggesting that the proper basis for philia is objective: those who share our dispositions, who bear no grudges, who seek what we do, who are temperate, and just, who admire us appropriately as we admire them, and so on. Philia could not emanate from those who are quarrelsome, gossips, aggressive in manner and personality, who are unjust, and so on. The best characters, it follows, may produce the best kind of friendship and hence love: indeed, how to be a good character worthy of philia is the theme of the Nicomachaen Ethics. The most rational man is he who would be the happiest, and he, therefore, who is capable of the best form of friendship, which between two "who are good, and alike in virtue" is rare (NE, VIII.4 trans. Ross). We can surmise that love between such equals-Aristotle's rational and happy men-would be perfect, with circles of diminishing quality for those who are morally removed from the best. He characterizes such love as "a sort of excess of feeling". (NE, VIII.6).

Friendships of a lesser quality may also be based on the pleasure or utility that is derived from another's company. A business friendship is based on utility-on mutual reciprocity of similar business interests; once the business is at an end, then the friendship dissolves. This is similar to those friendships based on the pleasure that is derived from the other's company, which is not a pleasure enjoyed for whom the other person is in himself, but in the flow of pleasure from his actions or humour.

The first condition for the highest form of Aristotelian love is that a man loves himself. Without an egoistic basis, he cannot extend sympathy and affection to others (NE, IX.8). Such self-love is not hedonistic, or glorified, depending on the pursuit of immediate pleasures or the adulation of the crowd, it is instead a reflection of his pursuit of the noble and virtuous, which culminate in the pursuit of the reflective life. Friendship with others is required "since his purpose is to contemplate worthy actions... to live pleasantly... sharing in discussion and thought" as is appropriate for the virtuous man and his friend (NE, IX.9).

The morally virtuous man deserves in turn the love of those below him; he is not obliged to give an equal love in return, which implies that the Aristotelian concept of love is elitist or perfectionist: "In all friendships implying inequality the love also should be proportional, i.e. the better should be more loved than he loves". (NE, VIII, 7,). Reciprocity, although not necessarily equal, is a condition of Aristotelian love and friendship, although parental love can involve a one-sided fondness.

Agape

Agape refers to the paternal love of God for man and of man for God but is extended to include a brotherly love for all humanity. (The Hebrew ahev has a slightly wider semantic range than agape). Agape arguably draws on elements from both eros and philia in that it seeks a perfect kind of love that is at once a fondness, a transcending of the particular, and a passion without the necessity of reciprocity. The concept is expanded on in the Judaic-Christian tradition of loving God: "You shall love the Lord your God with all your heart, and with all your soul, and with all your might" (Deuteronomy 6:5) and loving "thy neighbour as thyself" (Leviticus 19:18). The love of God requires absolute devotion that is reminiscent of Plato's love of Beauty (and Christian translators of Plato such as St. Augustine employed the connections), which involves an erotic passion, awe, and desire that transcends earthly cares and obstacles. Aquinas, on the other hand, picked up on the Aristotelian theories of friendship and love to proclaim God as the most rational being and hence the most deserving of one's love, respect, and considerations.

The Universalist command to "love thy neighbor as thyself" refers the subject to those surrounding him, whom he should love unilaterally if necessary. The command employs the logic of mutual reciprocity, and hints at an Aristotelian basis that the subject should love himself in some appropriate manner: for awkward results would ensue if he loved himself in a particularly inappropriate, perverted manner! (Philosophers can debate the nature of "self-love" implied in this-from the Aristotelian notion that self-love is necessary for any kind of interpersonal love, to the condemnation of egoism and the impoverished examples that pride and self-glorification from which to base one's love of another. St. Augustine relinquishes the debate-he claims that no command is needed for a man to love himself (De bono viduitatis, xxi.). Analogous to the logic of "it is better to give than to receive", the universalism of agape requires an initial invocation from someone: in a reversal of the Aristotelian position, the onus for the Christian is on the morally superior to extend love to others. Nonetheless, the command also entails an egalitarian love-hence the Christian code to "love thy enemies" (Matthew 5:44-45). Such love transcends any perfectionist or aristocratic notions that some are (or should be) more loveable than others. Agape finds echoes in the ethics of Kant and Kierkegaard, who assert the moral importance of giving impartial respect or love to another person qua human being in the abstract. However, loving one's neighbor impartially (James 2:9) invokes serious ethical concerns, especially if the neighbor ostensibly does not warrant love. Debate thus begins on what elements of a neighbor's conduct should be included in agape, and which should be excluded. Early Christians asked whether the principle applied only to disciples of Christ or to all.

The impartialists won the debate asserting that the neighbor's humanity provides the primary condition of being loved; nonetheless, his actions may require a second order of criticisms, for the logic of brotherly love implies that it is a moral improvement on brotherly hate. For metaphysical dualists, loving the soul rather than the neighbor's body or deeds provides a useful escape clause-or in turn the justification for penalizing the other's body for sin and moral transgressions, while releasing the proper object of love-the soul-from its secular torments. For Christian pacifists, "turning the other cheek" to aggression and violence implies a hope that the aggressor will eventually learn to comprehend the higher values of peace, forgiveness, and a love for humanity.

The universalism of agape runs counter to the partialism of Aristotle and poses a variety of ethical implications. Aquinas admits a partialism in love towards those we are related while maintaining that we should be charitable to all, whereas others such as Kierkegaard insisted on impartiality. Recently, Hugh LaFallotte (1991) has noted that to love those one is partial towards is not necessarily a negation of the impartiality principle, for impartialism could admit loving those closer to one as an impartial principle, and, employing Aristotle's conception of self-love, iterates that loving others requires an intimacy that can only be gained from being partially intimate. Others would claim that the concept of universal love, of loving all equally, is not only impracticable, but logically empty-Aristotle, for example, argues: "One cannot be a friend to many people in the sense of having friendship of the perfect type with them, just as one cannot be in love with many people at once (for love is a sort of excess of feeling, and it is the nature of such only to be felt towards one person)" (NE, VIII.6).

Added Conceptual Consideration

In aligned with Alexander Moseley, the logical conclusion, which implies that love has a nature is a proprosition that some may oppose with argument of its conceptually irrational. This is in the sense that it cannot be describe in a rational or meaningful propositions. For such critics are presenting a metaphysical and epistemology argument, which proposed love to be real or ideal in one hand, or an ejection of emotions or subconscious part of the mind that defy rational examination.

As solely presented by Moseley in the continuation of his work;

Presuming love has a nature, it should be, to some extent at least, describable within the concepts of language. But what is meant by an appropriate language of description may be as philosophically beguiling as love itself. Such considerations invoke the philosophy of language, of the relevance and appropriateness of meanings, but they also provide the analysis of "love" with its first principles. Does it exist and if so, is it knowable, comprehensible, and describable?

Love may be knowable and comprehensible to others, as understood in the phrases, "I am in love", "I love you", but what "love" means in these sentences may not be analyzed further: that is, the concept "love" is irreducible-an axiomatic, or self-evident, state of affairs that warrants no further intellectual intrusion, an apodictic category perhaps, that a Kantian may recognize. The epistemology of love asks how we may know love, how we may understand it, whether it is possible or plausible to make statements about others or ourselves being in love (which touches on the philosophical issue of private knowledge versus public behavior). Again, the epistemology of love is intimately connected to the philosophy of language and theories of the emotions. If love is purely an emotional condition, it is plausible to argue that it remains a private phenomenon incapable of being accessed by others, except through an expression of language, and language may be a poor indicator of an emotional state both for the listener and the subject.

Emotivists would hold that a statement such as "I am in love" is irreducible to other statements because it is a nonpropositional utterance, hence its veracity is beyond examination.

Phenomenologists may similarly present love as a non-cognitive phenomenon. Scheler, for example, toys with Plato's Ideal love, which is cognitive, claiming: "love itself... brings about the continuous emergence of ever-higher value in the object–just as if it were streaming out from the object of its own accord, without any exertion (even of wishing) on the part of the lover" (1954, p. 57). The lover is passive before the beloved.

The claim that "love" cannot be examined is different from that claiming "love" should not be subject to examination-that it should be put or left beyond the mind's reach, out of a dutiful respect for its mysteriousness, its awesome, divine, or romantic nature. But if it is agreed that there is such a thing as "love" conceptually speaking, when people present statements concerning love, or admonitions such as "she should show more love," then a philosophical examination seems appropriate: is it synonymous with certain patterns of behavior, of inflections in the voice or manner, or by the apparent pursuit and protection of a particular value ("Look at how he dotes upon his flowers-he must love them")? If love does possesses "a nature" which is identifiable by some means-a personal expression, a discernible pattern of behavior, or other activity, it can still be asked whether that nature can be properly understood by humanity. Love may have a nature, yet we may not possess the proper intellectual capacity to understand it-accordingly, we may gain glimpses perhaps of its essence-as Socrates argues in The Symposium, but its true nature being forever beyond humanity's intellectual grasp.

Accordingly, love may be partially described, or hinted at, in a dialectic or analytical exposition of the concept but never understood in itself. Love may therefore become an piphenomenal entity, generated by human action in loving, but never grasped by the mind or language. Love may be so described as a Platonic Form, belonging to the higher realm of transcendental concepts that mortals can barely conceive of in their purity, catching only glimpses of the Forms' conceptual shadows that logic and reason unveil or disclose.

Another view, again derived from Platonic philosophy, may permit love to be understood by certain people and not others. This invokes a hierarchical epistemology, that only the initiated, the experienced, the philosophical, or the poetical or musical, may gain insights into its nature. On one level, this admits that only the experienced can know its nature, which is putatively true of any experience, but it also may imply a social division of understanding-that only philosopher kings may know true love.

On the first implication, those who do not feel or experience love are incapable (unless initiated through rite, dialectical philosophy, artistic processes, and so on) of comprehending its nature, whereas the second implication suggests (though this is not a logically necessary inference) that the non-initiated, or those incapable of understanding, feel only physical desire and not 'love'.

Accordingly, "love" belongs either to the higher faculties of all, understanding of which requires being educated in some manner or form, or it belongs to the higher echelons of society-to a priestly, philosophical, or artistic, poetic class. The uninitiated, the incapable, or the young and inexperienced-those who are not romantic troubadours-are doomed only to feel physical desire.

Although, Moseley above explanation separated love from physical desire, therefore created further implications on the nature of romatic love. So he continues:

Nature of Love: Romantic love

Romantic love is deemed to be of a higher metaphysical and ethical status than sexual or physical attractiveness alone. The idea of romantic love initially stems from the Platonic tradition that love is a desire for beauty-a value that transcends the particularities of the physical body. For Plato, the love of beauty culminates in the love of philosophy, the subject that pursues the highest capacity of thinking. The romantic love of knights and damsels emerged in the early medieval ages (11th Century France, fine amour) a philosophical echo of both Platonic and Aristotelian love and literally a derivative of the Roman poet, Ovid and his Ars Amatoria. Romantic love theoretically was not to be consummated, for such love was transcendentally motivated by a deep respect for the lady; however, it was to be actively pursued in chivalric deeds rather than contemplated-which is in contrast to Ovid's persistent sensual pursuit of conquests!

Modern romantic love returns to Aristotle's version of the special love two people find in each other's virtues-one soul and two bodies, as he poetically puts it. It is deemed to be of a higher status, ethically, aesthetically, and even metaphysically than the love that behaviorists or physicalists describe.

To forge ahead, he also view love as issue of physical, emotional, and spirituality. Therefore, he placed his work in this form:

Some may hold that love is physical, i.e., that love is nothing but a physical response to another whom the agent feels physically attracted to. Accordingly, the action of loving encompasses a broad range of behavior including caring, listening, attending to, preferring to others, and so on. (This would be proposed by behaviorists). Others (physicalists, geneticists) reduce all examinations of love to the physical motivation of the sexual impulse-the simple sexual instinct that is shared with all complex living entities, which may, in humans, be directed consciously, sub-consciously or pre-rationally toward a potential mate or object of sexual gratification.

Physical determinists, those who believe the world to entirely physical and that every event has a prior (physical cause), consider love to be an extension of the chemical-biological constituents of the human creature and be explicable according to such processes. In this vein, geneticists may invoke the theory that the genes (an individual's DNA) form the determining criteria in any sexual or putative romantic choice, especially in choosing a mate.

However, a problem for those who claim that love is reducible to the physical attractiveness of a potential mate, or to the blood ties of family and kin which forge bonds of filial love, is that it does not capture the affections between those who cannot or wish not to reproduce-that is, physicalism or determinism ignores the possibility of romantic, ideational love—it may explain eros, but not philia or agape.

Behaviorism, which stems from the theory of the mind and asserts a rejection of Cartesian dualism between mind and body, entails that love is a series of actions and preferences which is thereby observable to oneself and others. The behaviorist theory that love is observable (according to the recognizable behavioral constraints corresponding to acts of love) suggests also that it is theoretically quantifiable: that A acts in a certain way (actions X,Y,Z) around B, more so than he does around C, suggests that he "loves" B more than C. The problem with the behaviorist vision of love is that it is susceptible to the poignant criticism that a person's actions need not express their inner state or emotions—A may be a very good actor. Radical behaviorists, such as B. F. Skinner, claim that observable and unobservable behavior such as mental states can be examined from the behaviorist framework, in terms of the laws of conditioning.

On this view, that one falls in love may go unrecognised by the casual observer, but the act of being in love can be examined by what events or conditions led to the agent's believing she was in love: this may include the theory that being in love is an overtly strong reaction to a set of highly positive conditions in the behavior or presence of another.

Expressionist love is similar to behaviorism in that love is considered an expression of a state of affairs towards a beloved, which may be communicated through language (words, poetry, music) or behavior (bringing flowers, giving up a kidney, diving into the proverbial burning building), but which is a reflection of an internal, emotional state, rather than an exhibition of physical responses to stimuli. Others in this vein may claim love to be a spiritual response, the recognition of a soul that completes one's own soul, or complements or augments it. The spiritualist vision of love incorporates mystical as well as traditional romantic notions of love, but rejects the behaviorist or physicalist explanations.

Those who consider love to be an aesthetic response would hold that love is knowable through the emotional and conscious feeling it provokes yet which cannot perhaps be captured in rational or descriptive language: it is instead to be captured, as far as that is possible, by metaphor or by music.[5]

---

5. Mind you that the foregoing topic: *"Nature of Love"* is a quoted work of Alexander Moseley. You can see footnote 3 and 4 for information about him.

The Laymen Meaning of Love

It is necessary to separate the Western view from that of laymen who are in the street. This is because, for a long time, people in the street have also searched for their own meaning of love, but the truth is that most of them understood it base on their feelings. For instance, to facilitate this work, in an online and offline survey of 30 adults comprising of 25 males and 5 females (in the marital status of 23 singles and, 7 married) that I conducted; people were given opportunity to think and put down their views on the meaning of love.

In response and result interpretation, 2 people agreed that there is no place where true love can be found, while 28 people said that true love exists, but 5 out of the 28 said it is of imaginary thing, while 23 said it is real. For example, below are most of the selected definitions:

"Love is having a passionate feeling, trust for another person and ready to die for the person." (A. Akin, Business Admin.)

"Love is having a strong or deep affection over somebody"
(D. Friday, Businessman)

"Love is being committed and trustful to something you desired"
(C. Kingsley, Pharmacist)

"Love is an emotion towards someone" (A. Amara, Student)

"Love is a characteristic that involves the exhibition of real tender feeling for somebody" (Paka, Biochemist)

"Love is a soul quality of a person we are attracted to"
(U. Wise, Safety officer)

"Love is showing compassion to someone close for you"
(J. Owen, Accountant)

"You will know the meaning of love when you fall in love"
(N. Samuel, Economist)
"Love is cherishing another person's ways of love" (A. Miller, Economist)

"Love is an act of endless forgiveness, a tender look which becomes a habit"
(Peter Ustinov)

"Love is an ideal thing, marriage a real thing.'' (Goethe)

"The question of love is one that cannot be evaded. Whether or not you claim to be interested in it, from the moment you are alive you are bound to be concerned with love, because love is not just something that happens to you: it is a certain special way of being alive. Love is, in fact, an intensification of life, completeness, fullness, a wholeness of life." (Thomas Merton)

In general point of view, many people feel love, but do not know the cause and meaning of it. The mostly common type of it we practiced is romantic love, which is a form of Eros. Moreover, most problems we experienced in our romantic relationship is because we do not know the cause of the prevailing force (which we called love) that is ruling our relationship. For example, we are common with such expressions like;

"He has treated me so badly since I met him, but I am still into this relationship because of the love I have for him."

"Some pitiful expression like "she does not worth having me, I don't know why I' m loving her."

The key point is that there is a difference between effect of love, and cause of love. Take for instance, for love to effect forgiveness does not mean that love is forgiveness, or it is forgiveness that causes love. Forgiveness can emerge because of pity. This is likewise caring. Love is caring as popularly says, but to care is not to love, as we believed. For instance, see this statement;

I can care about a person just for the sake of humanity, however not because I love the person or that the person possess some attractive intrinsic values. It can be out of pity or help, and such care can be transfered to a dog in exactly manner.

Due to this ignorance, sometimes, we are sick in our love relationship. Mainly for reciprocity, we mostly act foolishly because we thought that we are in love. At times, we break our guide; reject food because someone we love upset us, always dwelling on the receiving-end, enduring-and-tolerating-side, and living a life of nearest-to-endless forgiveness because we believed that love does not keep wrong. All these can be an attribute of misconception, for instance, our understanding that love is forgiveness, it is caring, tolerance, endurance, and it does not keep and count wrong. For instance, in most times, we have been jilted, beaten up, disgraced, and then afterward, we do returned to the relationship. However, for morality, we might accept that our response possesses character of foolishness, which can be attribute to _"I don't need a quarrel"_ attitude. If so, thus, love is as well "foolishness", probably "stupidity", and it can also be madness because most times we cannot control ourselves, and we go a little mad.

Nevertheless, is it love that drives us these ways? Yes, it is love, which has developed within frame of time, and known as _"compounded-feeling"_. Therefore, it is compounded-feeling that is responsible for;

- What causes love at first sight,
- Why people behaved foolishly and stupidly when they are in love,
- Why love dies off,
- Why love does not die,
- The limit we can control our love life, and
- Making dual loving impossible

In this point, if you understand this concept of compounded-feeling that we explained above, you will be able to answer and solve many psychological questions and problems constitute in your philosophy of love, love-relationship, or marriage.

The Rationale of Compounded-Feeling

The rationale of compounded-feeling, which I took time to derived as a concept stems from Harry W. Carpenter topic, *"The Brain"* in his book titled: *"The Power of Your Subconscious Mind"*, and the Platonic Traditional teaching, which sees *"love" as a desire for beauty- a value that transcends the particularities of the physical body.*

The platonic tradition is obvious because love involved the desire for beauty and/or value at its best form. However, in Harry W. Carpenter's work; for a better understanding, let us go through his teaching on the below topic:[6]

THE BRAIN

Most of you are familiar with the "Right-Brian, Left-Brian" Theory. Briefly, the left side of your brain (for most people) processsses language capability, thinks linearly, and is logical, whereas the right side of your brain is intuitive senses the whole, rather than parts.

Some experts believe this theory is an over simplification. Much of the research leading to this theory, at least initially, was obtained from epileptic patients who had the left and right sides of their brains surgically disconnected for medical reasons. In normal people, there is considerable feedback between both sides and, in special cases; one side can acquire the capabilities of the other. We will not use this model in this course.

We will consider the "Triune Model" of the brain developed by Dr. Paul MacLean, Chief of the Laboratory of Brain Research and Behavior, National Institute of Mental Health. The Triune model is based on three stages of evolution, the "Reptilian", "Mammalian", and "Cortex". Each stage represents a dfferent type of mentality geared to the needs that prevailed at the time. Each is a separate computer with its own special intelligence, subjectivity, sense of time and space, and memory. For our purposes, it is convenient to combine the first two parts, which are by far the oldest parts (the reptilian and mammalian parts) and call it the subcnscious mind.

---

6. "The Brain" is quoted from the book; "The Power of Your Subconscious Mind" (Harry W. Carpenter, 2005, pg 33-44)"

Reptilian

The first stage of the brain evolved 250 million years ago and is called the "reptilain brain", or the "brain stem". It stopped changing 250 million years ago. Thus, the reptilian brain in man is esssentially the same as in all reptiles. It is involuntary, impulsive, and compulsive; it contains programmed responses that are rigid. This part of the brain is paranoid for self-preservation. Paranoia is useful for keeping an eye out for enemies or, more to date, for cars when crossing the street. This part of the brain does not learn from experiences. It just tends to repeat its programmed behavior over and over.

The reptilian brain evolved for survival. It controls basic functions necessary for life including, heart rate, breathing, fighting, fleeeing, feeding, and reproduction. It has no feelings.

Mammalian

The mammalian brain evolved about 50 million years ago. The mammalian brain in man is also essentially the same as in all mammals. This part of the brain contains feelings and emotions. It is playful and the source of maternal care. Mammals tend to their young; reptiles usually do not.

The mammalian part of the brain provides us with feelings of what is real, true, and important to us, but it is inarticulate in commnicating these feelings to the conscious mind. Important features are that the subconscious mind (1) is the source of feelings and derives information in terms of feelings, and (2) derives its value system by experience, that is, experience with emotional impact.

Cortex

The third stage of development is the "cortex". It is the conscious part of the mind. According to Carl Jung, the famous psychiatrist, it is about 40, 000 years old and is still evolving. Some contemporary researchers think it is older. An important feature of the conscious mind is that it does not begin to develop until about age theree and is not fully developed until about 20 years of age. These ages vary between individuals.

This late development is one reason we have so many negative and counterproductive programs in our subconscious minds. When the emotional part of our brains was developing in the early years of our lives, we did not have a rational, mature conscious mind to filter out negative programs and select positive ones we will need as adults. To make matters worse, we are not aware of most of these programs now because they were developed at such an early age we have no conscious memory of them.

In contrast to the subconscious mind, which evolves its value system through emotions, the conscious mind evolves its value system through rational interpretation of experience. Because of these vast differences, "...the three brains are often dissociated and in conflict.

Ken Keys, author and lecturer, stated it well: "Although our cerebral cortex has more processing capacity than any computer ever built, unfortunately the new brain isn't wired into the old brain with the monitoring feedback, and control circuits that we need for optimal functioning. Thus the new brain, the conscious mind, will analyze problems and come up with rational solutions, often without the vaguest idea what is taking place in the old brain, the subconscious mind, which is governed by nonrational feeling... that is the crux of our problem. The poor communication between the old and new brains creates problems in everyday life. For example, the old brain can bypass the thinking brain's control systems and act out intense emotions that have been bottled up in the unconscious for decades...often making mountains out of molehills. The new brain, operating in present time, realizes that the person has strength, competence, and self-worth, yet the unconscious contnues to trigger ineffective, inappropriate responses to life's challenges based on negative childhood programmming."

The Difference between the Subconscious Mind and Conscious Mind

From the foregoing topic of the brain, the mammalian brain is responsible for the subconscious mind, while the cortex is of the conscious mind. However, there are differences between these two forms of mind, for better understanding, let us continued with Harry's teaching;

SIZE: The subconscious mind makes up an estimated 92% of the total brain. The conscious mind comprises the remaining 8%. Thus, the conscious mind is puny compared to the subconscious mind.

SIGHT: The conscious mind sees with the eyes. It perceives outside experiences that are taken into our minds. It is your conscious mind, which sees this printed page.

The sucbcoscius mind, on the other hand, has no contact with the outside world. It is blind. The subconscious mind does not see any more than a computer sees. Consequently, the subconscious mind does not know the difference between real and imagined. This last statement is important and will be repeated again and again. It is not conjecture; psychologists have verified it in laboratory experiments.

The subconscious mind relies on sensory input. Thus, it responds to reality and imagination in the same way. For example, when you dream of a monster, your body responds the same as it would if the monster were real. The "fight or flight" mechanism jumps into action and pumps adrenalin into your blood stream. Your body responds by sweating, increased heart rate, etc. In reality, there is no monster and no real threat.

COMMUNICATION: Most thoughts in the conscious mind are communicated by an inner or outer voice. Most, although not all, thinking uses a voice, and a voice uses words. The conscious mind communicates predominantly with words. That is one reason a large vocabulary is important. Words are the tools of thinking.

The subconscious mind has limited vocabulary and is not as articulate with words. Most people do not dream in words. The subconscious mind communicates predominantly with images and feelings. For example, you (your conscious mind) might say, "I am frightened, but I do not know why", while your subconscious mind might produce a dream in which a monster chases you.

FUNCTIONS: The conscious mind controls the voluntary functions. For example, I can consciously move my arm up or down. I can walk over here or there. These are conscious actions.

A critical factor is that the conscious mind can only do one thing at a time. It cannot do two things simultaneously. Someone may argue that they can read and watch TV at the same time. If you really become aware of what you are doing at an instant, you will see that you are either reading or watching TV. To do both requires that you quickly switch back and forth.

Recall the first time you tried to pat yourself on the top of your head and, at the same time, rub your stomach in a clockwise motion. You could not do it at first; not until you very quickly shifted one function to your subconscious mind. Then it became easy. Then when you were instructed to reverse the functions, that is, to rub the top of your head and pat your stomach, it again beame difficult. It may have only taken seconds to learn one function and relegate it to your subcnscious mind, in which case, doing both at the same time again became easy.

A recently article in the New York Times reported a scientific study that showed people cannot cosciously drive and talk on their cell phone at same time. In other words, you are doing one or the other cosciously, but not both simultaneously. Using magnetic resonance images of brain activity, the scientists found the brain has a finite amount of space for tasks requiring attention. One scientist commented that when you really want to listen to someone on the phone, you close your eyes.

Another article in a newspaper reported a mother who was so rapt in a cell phone conversation she got off the bus without her four-month-old baby.

A simple experiment will prove that your conscious mind can only do one thing at a time. Pick up a light object such as a pen. Will yourself to drop it. Easy! To drop the pen you have to make a conscious decision when to drop it. Now hold the pen and continue saying to yourself, "I can drop it; I can drop it..." on and on. If you truly concentrate on the one thought, the thought that you can drop the pen, then you cannot make the decision when to drop the pen. If you cannot make the decision when to drop the pen then you cannot drop it. You cannot continuously think, "I can drop the pen" and at the same time consciously think "Now, I will drop the pen."

Think about when you learned to drive a car. Many of us learned in a car with a stick shift. The first lesson went lik this. You turned the key. The car lurched and the engine died because we forgot to put the gear in neutral. You started the car again but it died because you did not give the engine more gas. You were thinking of turning the key. You started the car again and gave it some gas. You shifted gears only to hear a clash. You had forgotten to push in the clutch. Now you pushed down on the clutch pedal and shifted into first gear. You let off on the clutch and the engine died. You did not think to give it more gas. Finallly, the car started moving and your dad screamed, "Look out!" Oops, you were not steering; you were thinking of shifting gears.

Learning to drive is a good example of how difficult it is for the conscious mind to do many things at once. However, after you relegated one function after another to the subconscious mind, driving became easy-it no longer required conscious effort.

The subconscious mind, in contrast, can do trillions of functions at the same time. We do not have to conscientiously think to breathe, perspire when we are hot, digest our food, fight foreign bodies, release insulin, and on and on.

Your subconscious mind constantly communicates with all of the cells in your body, and the cells, in turn, communicate with your subconscious mind.

COGNITIVE PROCESS: The conscious mind is logical. It has the ability to think, think abstractly, reason, criticize, analyze, judge, choose, select, discriminate, plan, invent and compose, use hindsight and foresight. It uses both deductive and inductive reasoning. Your conscious mind, for the most part, filters the impact of input to the subconscious mind. Everything gets into the subconscious mind, but the conscious mind can influence the effect, or power, it has over the subconscious mind. As stated earlier, the conscious mind does not begin to develop until the age of three and it is not fully developed until about the age of 20. You did not have this filter during your critical, early formative years. Thus, you have a lot of garbage in your subconscious mind that is counterproductive to your health, peace of mind, and productivity. The subconscious mind, conversely, is not logical; it is the feeling mind. It is the source of love, hatred, anguish, fear, jealousy, sadness, anger, joy, desire, etc. When you say, "I feel..." the source of the feeling is the subconscious mind. Think of an extreme example, such as rage. A person expresssing deep rage exhibits strong emotion, superior strength, is highly illogical, and has poor (conscious) recollection of his or her carrying on afterward.

The subconscious mind reasons inductively, from the specific to general. If you tell it you are clumsy, it will find a way for you to do something clumsy. Usually inductive rationale is not logical.

The conscious mind thinks of words objectively. Objectively the word "mother" means a female parent. The subconscious mind, on the other hand, is subjective and adds connotations to words. When you hear the word "mother", all kinds of feelings are aroused. These feelings come from the subcnscious mind.

WILL, POWER, AND WILLPOWER: The conscious mind has a sense of awareness. It knows persons, places, conditions, and things. The conscious mind knows that it knows. It contains knowledge that we are ourselves and we are here.

Importantly the conscious mind has will. Will is the ability of the conscious mind to initiate and direct a thought or action. Will suppplies the direction of your thinking. Human beigns have free will.

Ah! But the subconscious mind has the power! An article in Psychology Today, August, 1974, stated that, "...we discovered the brain is a source of electrical energy; it can do electrical work". Your brain produces about 25 watts of power. The subconscious mind transmits this energy as urges, emtions, impulses, nervous twitches, etc.

This energy in the subconscious mind is inexhaustible; your brain functions 24-hours-a-day, all of your life. The wonderful thing about using the subconscious mind is that it is effortless. No conscious effort is required to use your subconscious mind. Conscious effort, no mattter how well intended, only impedes the subconscious mind requires effort.

Doing something with the conscious mind requires effort. Remember how learning something for the first time took effort? For example, it took a while to learn to tie a shoestring. It is complicated the first time or two. Imagine if you had to write out all the steps clearly enough so that someone who had never seen a bow could tie one.

Once tying a bow became habit-in other words, the task was relegated to the subconscious mind-it became easy. So easy, you do not have to think about it when you are doing it. In fact, you probably do not even remember tying the laces in your shoes because you did it subconsciously.

A high-jumper interviewed on TV after he set a track record said "I do not remember my record jump, but I knew when I started to jump that I would be successful". He did not remember because he was jumping unconsciously. He let his subconscious mind take over. The subconscious mind can do all the operations without mental effort. Had he jumped using his conscious mind, it would have been an effort and he would not have done nearly as well.

The best book on this subject is "The Inner Game of Tennis by Timothy Gallwey". Do not be turned off by the title if you are not a tennis player; just mentally cross out "tennis" as you read and insert any other word you want Gallwey articulately describes how the conscious mind cannot do a task as difficult as hitting a tennis ball (or driving a car or hitting a golf ball) well. Whereas, the subconscious mind can do a difficult task, and do it effortlessly and perfectly when not interfered with the conscious mind. That is the trick-keeping the conscious mind out of the way.

So, the conscious mind has the will and the subconscious mind has the power. When the conscious mind and subconscious mind are in harnony, you have willpower. You are "single-minded".

But when the conscious mind and subconscious mind are in conflict, there is no willpower. You "double-minded". Your conscious mind cannot directly overpower you subconscious mind and "will" it to do something.

Your task is to learn how the subconscious mind works and use it to your advantage. The subconscious mind has the power to dominate, but it is not as smart as your conscious mind.

MEMORY: The conscious mind has a limited memory and most of it is short-term. The subconscious mind, in stark contrast, has virtually infinite memory. You are probably thinking it does not seem that way to you. Well, it is true. You have enough memory for everything you have experienced in your life. It is your recall that is fallible.

CONTROL: When your conscious mind and your subconscious mind are in conflict, your subconscious mind wins, but only if you do not know how to control it.

In this life, it is very important for us to learn how to influence and control our subconscious mind so that it does not control us. Harry Carpenter went far in his work emphasising that; the conscious mind, which is the master, can control the subsconscious mind, which in turn the genie. He stated:

> *"The conscious mind can stimulate the subconscious mind into action, change habits, reverse negative thinking patterns, improve our physical and emotional health, and our conscious mind can even influence our invlountary functions. (Harry W. Carpenter, 2005, pg 44)"*

To further his teaching, he explained the four states of mind, which are alpha, beta, theta, and delta. According to him[7]

STATES OF THE MIND

Using your subconscious mind effectively requires being in an Alpha state of mind. This altered state is natural, but it is different from your normal awake state of mind. The first proof of the need to use an altered state to access the subconscious mind, as far as I know, was demonstrated by the work of Elmer and Alyce Green at the Menninger Foundation from 1964 to 1973. The husband-wife duo studied individuals who did what seemed, at the time, superhuman feats. They studied, among others, Indian fakirs while they were buried alive for six days, laid on a bed of nails, or changed their heart rates and body temperatures. They stuudied Jack Schwarz, of Oregon, while he pierce himself through the arm with unsterilized metal rods. Schwarz controlled his bleeding, never became infected, and the wounds healed rapidly without leaving a mark. The Greens measured such things as body temperature, skin resistance, blood pressure, pulse, and brain waves.

These subjects had one thing in common while they performed these extraordinary feats: they were in altered states of mind.

There are four states of mind, beta, alpha, theta, and delta, and they are distinguished by a change in brain waves measured by an electrocephalograph.

Beta

The beta state is our normal awake state and is characterized by a brain wave frequency of 14cps (cycles per second) to 100 cps. Not only is the frequency higher than other states, it is more erratic. This is because our awake mind is busy. We are of many things that are going on around us. This awareness is essential for conducting our daily business and survival. Our attention constantly drifts. We are in the beta state most of our awake hours.

Alpha

The alpha state is characterized by a brain wave frequencny of 8 to 13 cps. You naturally go into the alpha state many times each day, but ususallly only fleetingly. Occasionally you may hover in this state. You would recognize it as daydreaming. Perhaps at one time or another you became bored, for example, standing in a slow line. You stared but your concentration was not on the thing you were staring at. Your mind was someplace else. You were in alpha. The alpha state is referred to as the "meditative"state-a state of relaxed, focused concentration. When you are in this state, you lose track of time. You may have stared at the wall for five minutes, but you think, incorrectly, you were staring at the wall for only a few seconds.

Theta

The theta state (4 to 7 cps) is similar to the alpha state but deeper and characterized by sudden intuitive insights. These insights are global. A classic example of global insight is comparing the way Beethoven and Mozort composed music. Beethoven composed linearly, measure by measure, often going back and forth changing notes. Mozart said that a composition would come to him all at once and in entirety. All he had to do was to write it down on paper. That is the epitome of global thinking.

Delta

Last is the delta (3 cps and lower.) This is the sleep state in which there is no consciousness. Dreaming occurs in the alpha and theta states.

Among the states of the mind, the alpha condition is the state, where we can program how the conscious mind control the subconcisous mind.

7."*The State of Mind*" is quoted from the book;"*The Power of Your Subconscious Mind*" (Harry W. Carpenter, 2005, pg 22-24)".

Alpha Conditioning

For how to program the conscious mind to be in control of the subconscious mind, Harry continues in his work;

To use your subconscious mind effectively, you need to learn to go into the alpha state at will and stay there. Going into alpha is easy. You naturally go into it many times each day, albeit, usually only for seconds. It takes a little practice to go into the alpha or theta state at will and stay there.

Hypnopompic and Hypnagogic Periods
These are just fancy names for the short periods when you wake in the morning and fall asleep in the evening. When you wake in the morning and when you fall asleep at night, you go from delta to beta and beta to delta states, respectively. As you do, you passs through the alpha and theta states. So twice each day you have an opportunity to program your sbuconscious mind while in the alpha state. This is also why you should never go to bed while worrying. Worry is powerful affirmation and you would be implanting this powerful, negative affirmation directly into your subconscious mind. (Harry W. Carpenter, 2005, pg 25)

"Your mind can be led into the alpha state by sitting in comfortable chair and listening to a relaxation routine read by someone else, or recorded and played back. The routine usually takes about ten minutes. You will want to go into the alpha state many times each day to give your genie instructions. It would not be practical to depend on someone else to read the routine, or to play a CD every time you wanted to go into alpha. You need to condition yourself by simply taken a deep breath, count down from three to one, say to yourself the word "ALPHA", and be in alpha. It is quick and that simple-after you are conditioned.

Alpha conditioning is easy. It just takes a little practice. Some people can condition themselves in a few sessions; others induce alpha. Relaxation is often associated with heaviness and warmth. Once in alpha, you condition yourself to return to this state quckly any time you want."
(Harry W. Carpenter, 2005, pg 45-46)

From the foregoing, it is possible to program your life to the point, where the subconscious mind, which is the genie, will be under the control of the conscious mind, which is the master in the *alpha state* of your mind. It is in this state, you can give instruction to the subconscious mind concerning your love life, and relationship. Examples of such instruction include instructing your subconscious mind things you will no longer like to do, things you may like doing, or even things you are expecting to get, and all will workout that way.

Generally, from the above works of Harry Carpenter, and Plato, we can draw a logical inferences; stating the causes of love to be desire, thought, experience, and feeling within the contents of the mind (i.e., the conscious and subconscious mind).

So love as a desire for beauty- a value that transcends the particularity of the physical body can originate from thought and experience, reflected so long in the mind and turned to feeling, thus, began to stimulate actions as results on behaviour. In other way, it is a **compounded feeling** formed by much passionate desires, thought, and experiences for one's choice of beauty and value on a particular person.

In aligned with Helen Fisher[8], this feeling runs in the stages of **lust**, **attraction**, and **attachment**. In these forms, lust is the passionate sexual desire that promotes mating. Attraction is the appealing quality that magnetics one to another, and attachment is the emotional bond that binds two people who attracted themselves together. Obviously, behind, every particularity noticed in a love-relationship, there is existence of these three stages.

Mind you, that this is why we do not succeed in trial relationship, until we found that person possessing our desiring particularity; we will not fall in love. Once a person meets the actual person, beyond the person's effort, the subconcious mind will activate a love scene. It is an involuntary action and attitude.

Normally, to be in romantic love is to activate the desired and observed peculiar intrinsic and extrinsic values of someone admired, by being obsessed and intoxicate about them within the work of the subconscious mind to a large extent.

---

8. Helen Fisher is an expert in the topic of love, in one of her work; she divided love into three stages, which are lust, attraction, and attachment. **See** http://en.wikipedia.org/wiki/Helen_Fisher_%28anthropologist%29

Remember that our subconscious mind has no value judgment character, which is unlike the conscious mind. Once it accepted a value placed on any thing through the information passed to it by the conscious mind, so it shall remain until the information will be reprogrammed or replaced by other information or concept. This is why in most times, when we give up an existing relationship, we may suffer a heartbreak, but with time fall in love with another person.

For effect, the above concept plays an acknowledged impact on why sometimes we behave irrational in our romantic relationship. For instance, in a situation where a person falls in love (as we often said), thus been maltreated, the conscious mind, which is judgmentally sensitive, will evaluate the situation and give options like:

- *do not allow him or her to be treating you this way,*
- *quit the relationship if he/she does not change for better,*
- *reciprocate positively, and others as the case may be,*

However, the subconscious mind, which is judgmentally insensitive, like playing a roll of a film, will replay the dominant concept, which most times covering all the periods when the relationship was moving without hitches, and as well reminding you those things you like about the person, thus calling your proposed revenge actions to be retreated.

Although, one thing to know about this situation is that, once you are in this mood, you may loose your willpower relative to that person you love.

The question remains, why is the subconscious mind responding this way? Okay! Remember our studies on the four states of the mind, which are the *beta, alpha, theta, and delta.* Most times in our lives, our love experience or events such as; going to beach party, having good sexual intercourse, saying love words to each other, good way of sharing problems, being together and all forms of affection are internalized into the subconscious mind during the period of our alpha state.

Remember that the Alpha state period involves an act of making our experience and attitudes such as love experience, love feelings, love belief, etc to be fully part of our personality, by absorbing them through meditation or self imagination into the subconscious mind. This internalization process makes the subconscons mind not to be judgemental. This is not only in love issues, but also in general issues. Therefore, those who said that "Love" is blind, madness, sickness, foolishness, forgiveness, insensible, etc are not far from their experiences.

Although, there may be incidents of exceptional cases, where the victim cannot debug these stored programs, thus the person will find it hard to give up the relationship. What happened to people who suffered exceptional cases is that, they have spent greater part of their time in meditating and imagining their ideal person particularity, and past love experience, therefore often stay in their world of ecstasy. This is why in such case; they cannot get ride of the experience, since the love experience cannot easily be replace or delete because no space is free for other image or information to occupy.

Moreover, if you are in this situation, the better decision is to look for a second choice partner. However, if you do not have, you can give room for another relationship. Open your mind and develop feeling for the new person entirely. In assertiveness, encourage yourself with statement such as "_I love him/her_". In addition, meditate and imagine those qualities you like about the person, spend time together with the person, and if possible take shopping and loving spree together. By doing all these activities together, you may debug the existing programs (images or information) of the former person out of your mind, and replace them with the newer events you had with the new person.

Alternatively, concentrate with your life, be focus in other things you are doing, perhaps your career and as time goes, you will be free. Never mind, what may be of the condition as the transition goes with time. However, the above explanation is why most times you hear someone saying,

> _"I don't believe that I can forget every thing about him/her. During our relationship, I so much loved him or her, but now the whole issue is forgotten, and I do not know if she or he still exists._

The Laws of Subconscious mind[9]

From the work of Harry W. Carpenter, the following laws of subconscious mind informed us how to communicate issues from the conscious side of our mind into the subconscious mind. The laws include, the law of Repetition, Emotion, Present tense, One-dominant-concept, Expectation, and Reverse-effort.

Repetition: *New programs accepted by the subconscious mind must be nurtured. When programming the subconscious mind, it is necessary to repeat the conditioning often until it is totally accepted by the subconscious mind. After it is accepted, the program should be repeated periodically to ensure that it remains dominant.*

Emotion: *Attaching emotion to a suggestion makes it more effective. Emotion is the power in the subconscious mind. You must use it when programming your subconscious mind to be successful.*

Present tense: *The conscious mind lives by time, namely past, present, and future, whereas the subconsicou mind only lives in the present. In the subconscious mind, the past is merely present recollections and the futre is present predictions.*

One Dominant Concept: *The subconscious mind will acccept only one concept to be true at any time. More than one concept (thought, habit, and program) can be held in the subconsicous mind at the same time, but only one will be binding. Thus, when the subconscious mind recognizes a concept as true, that concept guides and dominates you actions.*

The subconscious mind will only give up on the dominant concept when a stronger, opposing concept is impressed on it. The significance is that concept cannot be eliminate, it is imbedded in your subconscious mind, and your subconscious mind does not forget. A negative concept must be overpowered with a stronger, positive one. The good news is that the source of the concept does not have to be known; it just has to be overpowered with a positive one.

Expectation: *The subconscious mind is like a goal seeking computer. Whatever goals are supplied, the subconscious mind seeks to fulfill them. A sincere expectation is a goal given to your subconscious mind, and the law can be stated: When the subconscious mind expects something, it makes that thing happen.*

Reverse Effort: *You cannot sleep. The more determined you are to sleep, the more you wake up.*

---

9. "The Law of Subconscious Mind" is quoted from the book;
"The Power of Your Subconscious Mind" (Harry W. Carpenter, 2005, pg 79-95)"

Instance of Love at first Sight

"Thoughts which are mixed with any of the feelings of emotions constitute a "magnetic" force which attracts other similar or related thoughts. (Napoleon Hill, 1963, pg 35)

Take another instance, the incident of love at first sight, which is a case where the passionate desire of a particular person, typically sexual passion and other qualities are magneted by another person's desire at first sight.

In this case, the particularity (i.e. the peculiar extrinsic and intrinsic values) of the attracted person must have been desired, had as a thought, and reflected on for a long time before the unexpected meeting. That is to say, the *peculiar intrinsic values* such as *the natural physical outlook, way of speaking, social attitude,* et cetera, and the *peculiar extrinsic values such as social status, career level, academic qualification, mode of dressing, religion, parental background,* et cetera, must have been observed, thought of, reflected on via imagination, and built with a mental picture for a very long time before the encounter.

So how does the temperament of love at first sight get developed? One thing to remember is that in life, we all have different value systems as well as passionate desires. Take for instance, your passionate desiring ideal man or woman quality may be good physical-looking (perhap, a fair one indeed), and intelligent person, (i.e. base on your value system), and within you lies the power to desire, thought and feel these particularities or qualities in any period of time (especially in the alpha state).

Now in the process of the desiring, there are imaginations and expectation running as fantasy that one day, you may come across such person. So in most period of your life as activities go on including sleeping, relaxation, dreaming, et cetera, you will be in the situations to program (i.e. download) this ideal person particularity or qualities into the subconscious mind, expecially in your Alpha state. Eventually as you come across such person, your subconscious mind will stimulate this particularity or qualities through the power of emotion, then admiration will take effect.

The Mind and Computer System Analogy

We should know that our mind is sensitive to our sensory input factors, relative to our thinking, seeing, and imagination. Like a computer, it constitutes both the Random Access Memory, **RAM** (*the memory part of a computer that store information when computer is on, and delete information when the computer is off.*), and Read Only Memory, **ROM** (it is *like the RAM, but keep information even when the computer is shutdown*).

By analogy, the RAM stored our temporary life experiences, which in most cases we often forget. This is because most of these experiences are not subconscious in state. For example, the face of unknown person, you just saw in a Magazine. The ROM in the other hand holds the experiences we cannot forget, and most of these experiences are subconscious in state, and can be develop in alpha state period. For instance anything we visualize, say, and think repeately or reflected on so long or imagined constructively will be saved in the subconscious part of our mind, thus hardly to forget or delete. For example, you cannot forget how the face of your mother or father looks like.

Relatively, your passionate desire for someone, when reflected on so long, and imagined constructively will lead to thought, from thought to feeling and expectation, thus to *compounded feeling* (or love as you may call it).

The same process of internalization goes with all general temperament, experiences, as they can be store in the subconscious part of the mind. Although, from all we have learnt, we can say;

> *Love is a compounded feeling formed by compounded passionate desires, thought, and expereicne for one's choice of beauty and value(s) on the particularity of a person or a thing.*[10]

From the above definition, the development of love is based on issue of time frame, and its power is emotion. The emotion ejects the feelings in respond to our actions. This is why it is beyond our control because the feelings are conveyed into our subconcious mind through the conscious part.

Moreover, it is also from this point that Helen Fisher grouped the occurring stages of love relationship into three stages, which are *lust, attraction, and attachment*. Meaning that in a domain of compounded feelings, when we meet a corresponding person, the first passion to emerge is lust, attraction, and then lastly, the attachment, which is that stage where the longevity of the love relationship resides.

---

10 That is my position about the definition of love.

The Failed of Dual Loving Temperament

Conventional wisdom has taught us that loving pattern, which is our self-loving style can be of dual or single loving. By dual loving, we are referring to an act of loving two the same-sex in equal proportion at the same time. Take for example, the possiblity of a man loving two the same woman at equal proportion.

Now the question remains, is it possible to love two the same sex persons at a time in equal proportion? The answer may be 'yes or no' depending on a person.

Critically, those who believed in dual loving with a proper knowledge are holding an assumption that the actor (the lover) has programmed the particularities of two different persons he or she loves into his/her subconscious mind during the alpha state period. But, this is not possible despite the infinity storage capacity of the subconscious mind.

The allocated (occupying) space for a concept, information, or image to be accepted as true in the subconsicous mind is like a *'tabula rasa'* (a Latin word meaning clear tablet), once a particular concept, or image is saved on it, it will not be possible to save another. That is, once the particularity of a particular person is saved in the likeness of image or concept, the possibility to save another is only when the former is deleted within a period.

Supportively, the *law of one-dominant-concept* we studied previously, which stated; *"the subconscious mind would only accept one concept to be true at any time,"* supports this viewpoint. Therefore, whenever the subconscious mind recognizes a concept as true, that concept guides and dominates our actions. In other words, once the subconscious mind recognizes the particularity of a particular person as true, that particularity guides and dominates the actions of the person.

The Benfits of the Proposition

If you understand what we have learnt so far, you can be able to apply these few words of wisdom[11] that are stated below:

✓ *Within you lies the power in your mind in which when properly grasped and directed, it can prevent you out of any heartbreak, or lovelorn.*

✓ *You must control the deepest perception of what you feel, least you will be overwhelmed by the forces of that feeling.*

✓ *Within you lies the power to change your love feeling.*

✓ *You are a minute expression of your feeling and as such, you have no forceful feeling except those accepted by your mind.*

✓ *Your mind is like a fertile field, it will return anything planted into it. For examples, with strong affirmation such as " I love her/him " and cannot stay without her/him " then you will love and will not be able to stay without.*

✓ *Everything you see began as idea on the mind. The beauty of the woman, which you see is nothing more than the lingering evidence of that which has already taken place in your mind as thought.*

✓ *One thing about admiration is that it is of choice, you may love your friend as you claimed, but you can neither force the person to reciprocate, nor force your desire on the person.*

✓ *Do not think love to be of a reciprocity or you will always be at the complaining-side when you give and do not receive.*

---

11. I coined these Words of Wisdom from that of Napolean Hill, 1963.

INFATUATION AND LOVE (EROS)

There is a thin line between infatuation and love in the perspective of eros. There are questions such as "Are you in love or infatuation?"

Although, I am not confronting the existence of infatuation in romantic relationship, but the mentioned symptoms, biological, and the mindset causes of infatuation, which many love experts believed as the causes.

In the existence of life, experience has shown that most people do not fall to romantic relationship approach at the sensitive of some feeling of panic, overwhelming lust, feverish excitement, jealously, et cetera. Take for instance, some of the usual sayings include:

- *I don't think he is in love, may be it is infatuation.*
- *He is infatuated because of my beauty.*

What is Infatuation?

Infatuation can been seem as a state of having a strong passion for person in a manner where it will prevent the affected person from thinking in a balanced and sensible way over the admiring person. In other way, you are infatuated, if your thinking state over a person is imbalanced and insensible.

Some people have attributed body chemical reaction, loneliness, physical attraction, need for attention, and others as the cause of it. One of these persons is Ningthoujam Sandhyarani[12] who stated that:

> *Physical attraction happens to be one of the biggest reasons for a person falling for somebody. Physical beauty attracts you, and you feel like being physically close to that special person.[12]*

Moreover, some love experts believed that when someone 'claims' to be in love, some symptoms can be used as measures to conclude if that person is truly in love. Such person is Harry Croft[13] who agreed that the following symptoms are signs of infatuation; feeling of panic, overwhelming lust, feverish excitement, and jealousy.

---

12. By Ningthoujam Sandhyarani on (http://www.buzzle.com/articles/causes-of-infatuation.html). Last updated January 22, 2013.
13. Harry Croft is the Medical Director, (Psychyiatrist) of Healthy Place. See www.healthyplace.com, Last update on June 1, 2009

Furthermore, both Ningthoujam Sandhyarani[12], and Harry Croft[13] shared the same view on the biological cause of infatuation.

A likely cause behind infatuation is the chemical reactions that take place in your brain. When you see a person you like, phenylethylamine (PEA), a natural alkaloid, is emitted by your body, which speeds up the communication between your nerve cells and triggers the release of dopamine, which creates a feeling of bliss.[12]

When infatuated we experience a surge of dopamine that rushes through the brain causing us to feel good. Norepinephrine flows through the brain stimulating production of adrenaline (pounding heart). Phenylethalimine (found in chocolate) creates a feeling of bliss. Irrational romantic sentiments may be cause by oxytocin, a primary sexual arousal hormone that signals orgasm and feelings of emotional attachment. Together these chemicals sometimes override the brain activity that governs logic.[13]

In this work, however, the argument is not against the biological cause-effect of infatuation, but we can hold '*illusion*' such as false belief, false idea, or wrong perspective responsible. Sometimes they can misinformed us, thus over falsified the desire particularity of a person thereby making us to develop an *illusory particularity or behaviour* on the person, and as well as putting us in illusory state of mind, which affect the brain in reactions.

Relatively, it is this illusory state of mind (or mindset), which affect the brain in reaction that perhaps produces the above stated biological cause-effect. This is because both love and infatuation reflecting to our attitudes are of brain origination, and the brain constitutes the mind, which is conscious and subconscious in nature.

One thing we should learn is an illusory state of mind can be disillusion, thus, every false belief, idea, perspective, or misinformation will be well informed, and at this point, the feelings that were developed during the get together or at the first meeting may serve as the bedrock of the relationship.

However, as we mentioned earlier, we can condition infatuation as a state where one thinking is insensible. But, we may ask, is it the same condition when we say, "love is blind?" Yes, this is because the power of subconscious mind is inclusive, and if you believe in our 'concept of compounded feeling', then understand that, it is the same internalization process leading to love, which also lead to infatuation.

---

12. By Ningthoujam Sandhyarani on (http://www.buzzle.com/articles/causes-of-infatuation.html).Last updated January 22, 2013.
13. Harry Croft is the Medical Director, (Psychyiatrist) of Healthy Place. See www.healthyplace.com, Last update on June 1, 2009

Therefore, in the likeness of eros as a scope, there is interplay between them (love and infatuation) as both of them share the same symptoms and feelings with no perfect demarcation.

Despite this, some love experts still believe in the distinct symptoms of infatuation. Such person for example is still someone like Ningthoujam Sandhyarani[12], who expressly outlined some symptoms of infatuation such as feeling of panic, overwhelming lust, feverish excitement, jealously, thrilled, not-happy, wanting-to-be-trust, always-suspicious, and nagging.

There is no denial in the existence of the symptoms, but we can as well experience them even in the midst of love relationship.

Feeling of panic: you can love someone with a mix feeling of panic. The ability to love is a one sided-attitude, and you are in love because the loved person possesses your passionate desires. In a situation, where you wish not to loose your lover, panic may result due to fear of insecurity. This is because you can be in love with a person, but cannot force the person to love you in return. Therefore, the feeling of panic due to fear of insecurity does not mean you are not in love. Moreover, fear is natural and its occurrence is as well natural. The major difference is on your form of concern. Sometimes we developed fear in our romantic relationship, but why been afraid? We cannot really hit the point, may be it is insecurity and/or other factors, yet we are in love.

Overwhelming lust: My first question is, in which form of love relationship is overwhelming lust will be pronounce? A relationship built by agape? No, but a romantic relationship, which is a form of relationship, where sex is the one key element that distinguishes it from all other types, and one of the ways to express love is through sexuality, thus a lover is predispose to sexual desire toward a partner.

In addition, what is lust? In synonymize to sex, it is a strong physical desire to have sex with a person, usually with or without associated feelings of love. An *overwhelming lust* is when there is a higher degree of desire to have sex with person. Irregularity of sexual indulgence (or sex starve) in most romantic relationship can cause overwhelming lust. For instance, a person who may not have had sex with a partner either for the first or second time can be overwhelmed by lust at a particular point in time. Therefore, strong sexual physical desire can be found both in the state of love and infatuation.

The hypothesis that there is a positive correlation between *regular sexual intercourse* and *rosy romantic relationship* has to be in consideration. This is why most times we have hitches due to lack of sexual intercourse in our marriage or relationship.

Feverish excitement: Excitement is natural when it comes to enthusiasm. Love fever can stimulate feverish excitement. Meaning that someone can be feverishly excited due to love fever. What is love fever? It is a great enthusiasm over love. That is a person's strong passionate desire over a loved one or something can transmute the person's interest into excitement at any confrontation. There is a fact that we normally get excited at any moment we are together with a loved one. In some occasions, the intensity of the excitement depends; may be how long we have been missing each other before the meeting.

Jealousy: Whether it is infatuation or love, the fact is in every romantic relationship, there is existence of jealousy. What is jealousy? In this context, it is a natural phenomenon, and possessive feeling in us, harboured against suspicious rival influence, especially regarding to our relationship. We only jealous what we love, and so it is in the scripture that our Maker is a Jealous God[14], simply because He loves us.

Impact of the Concept

Nevertheless, many relationships that could have blossomed into lasting marriage have been destroyed due to our wrong perspective concerning love and infatuation. We are conversant with comments like:

> *Does he really love her? I think this is infatuation not actually love.*

Moreover, like Ningthoujam Sandhyarani also said:

> *"Lack of true love between two people is also a major cause of infatuation. As time goes by, one gets to know about the true nature of his love. Many times, you reach a saturation point or certain stagnation in your relationship. At this point of time, you start looking for someone else in your life. This is when you get infatuated, either because the new person possesses qualities that your partner lacks, or simply because you need a temporary change."*

Contrarily, this may be in the different view with Helen Fisher's stages of love. For example, a situation where love relationship has passed the stage of lust, and attraction, which are the first and second stages respectively, then finally, exists or get hold on the weakness of the third stage (i.e. attachment). Can we say the relationship broke up due to infatuation? No, rather the transmutation of such relationship is a movement from stage to stage, due to chemical reactions in the body system in one hand, and in the other hand, including some factors, which we will study later.

---

14. Deuteronomy 5:9

The truth is that the *"attitude to find out whether a person's feeling is infatuation or love"* should be thrown into a dustbin. Love is love. There is no love relationship where you cannot find the existence of any of the above-mentioned symptoms of infatuation. There are thousands of relationships where those symptoms have existed, yet those relationships are still alive, and most of them are in good marriages, and rosy romantic form.

For a better relationship, the need to find out, whether someone's feeling for you is love or infatuation is not a necessary condition or sufficient condition, rather it is a complication. This is because by dwelling on such thought to confirm whether the person's feeling towards you is infatuation or love, you may get yourself confused. The best is to open up, and observe the person, that is if you have interest because there is a thin line between love and infatuation.

Chapter Two

BEYOND LOVE RELATIONSHIP

Introduction

The forces behind movement of this world is in the forces of relationship among all elements. For instance, the relationship force between God and man, interpersonal relationship among persons, love relationship in married and unmarried, and other forms of relationship not mentioned. Beside this, the issue of relationship is necessary and worth learning, observing and practising in every endeavour of life. It is a necessity and makes life flows. As the world moves on, everything is in relationship. For example, in societal point of view, we are compulsive in nature to relate with one another, the Infinite Being (Almighty God), and our surrounding environment. In other words, there are relationships between man and his environment, and as well man and God. Moreover, there is functional relationship that shows the way in which certain things, events, ideas, et cetera, either in variables or in constants relates.

However, in this chapter, we will learn most of the issues about _Love relationship (LR)_ and, outlined some benefits of the topic. Although, most of these issues are beyond and out of common knowledge, but if you have followed the previous chapter, you may over come the challenges of it. The only action required is a _self-questioning mind approach_ over the new knowledge that you may gain from the learning, and this must be achieved through the instrumentality of _personal deep thought._

Nevertheless, the essence of this chapter is to take a beyond view of the phenomenon called _"Love relationship"_. The hidden motives behind every love relationship, the psychological states surrounding it, why some relationship survived, and some did not. In addition, how to understand our love personality type, including our partner's love personality type, having a better view of the relationship commitment, how we can make and select a good partner, what to know in order to protect ourselves in any love relationship and others as we proceed.

Expectation

At the end of this chapter, you expected to understand your personality love type, including whys and answers of many circumstances and characters found in love relationships, which were beyond our common knowledge. For instance, why your partner is behaving that way to you, why such response from you, why your love relationship is in such conditions, why people you love do not love you in return, and others.

WHAT IS LOVE RELATIONSHIP?

It is an association between two or more people based on human interaction, which involves the expression of love through intimacy without exploitation and manipulation. A good example of love relationship is *romantic relationship (RR)*, which exists in a couple, both married and unmarried ones.

From the above, our emphasis is on romantic relationship (RR), which is when two people share a deep feeling of being connected. They see themselves as one, accept themeselves the way they live, often feel good and happy when being together. They deeply appreciate each other, and live on a union interest rather than individual interest.

You can only find a true RR between lovers (i.e. married and unmarried people) only if they fit into each other preferred life partner, in relation to particularity, career goals, beliefs and value systems, most cases ethnicity, and other factors. Although, there are forms of RR and they do not exist in the same manner, but may exist towards one intent or goal. For formation, most of them are being formed out of personal choice relating to the prevailing environment, and while some are of natural choice. However, beyond self-control, there are visible and invisible forces that can make a person jump into RR for a period of interval, in some cases to assess the person first before involvement, or to accept due to indirect persuasion as time goes on.

Forms of RR

RR does not just emerge, it must have a cause before its effect. Most times people indulged into relationships because of problems of need, in search of love, out of compensation, or due to illusory mindset. For instance, it is common to hear some sayings like these:

- *I'm disappointed in this relationship.*
- *I don't know why, I'm into this kind of relationships.*
- *I'm into this relationship because he has been a good help to my situations.*
- *I'm into this relationship out of pity.*
- *I am happy in this relationship because he is my ideal person.*

Moreover, many people are into unhappy relationship, while some are into happy ones. Although, there is no natural or universal law governing the principles of reciprocity in love relationship, so if you are not happy with your relationship, try to be happy, take a deep thought and study concerning the love personality type of your partner and yourself, and for solution. The problem may be from the 'stilt' that is holding the relationship.

LOVE RELATIONSHIP INDUCTION

Every romantic relationship has a paranormal force,
which functions as the relationship stilt. The stilt is
the foundation that makes its existence stand.

It is unfortunate that many do not know how to freeze out of trouble or 'no-longer-interested' RR. However, knowing the cause that underpins a RR could enable an affected person to act whenever it becomes unbearable. Therefore, it is necessary to look into factors that can induce a RR. These factors are elements or reasons why people formed RR. I personally specified them as *illusion-induced, model-induced,* and *need-induced relationship.*

Illusion-Induced

Illusion is the deceptive power of appearances, that is, the ability of appearances to deceive the mind and senses, or the capacity of the mind and senses to be deceived by appearances.[15]

An illusory mindset can play somebody falsely; thus, make the person perceived particularity of a targeted person falsely in his or her mind. In this manner, according to most encyclopedia[16], it will become a psychology mistaken sensory perception, that is, a misinterpretation of an experience of sensory perception, especially a visual one, where the stimuli are objectively present and the mistaken perception is due to physical rather than psychological causes.

---

15. See Microsoft® Encarta® 2009. © 1993-2008 Microsoft Corporation. All rights reserved.
16. Like that of the Microsoft® Encarta® 2009. © 1993-2008 Microsoft Corporation.

By nature, RR induced by illusion never last, as the actors often get disappointed of each other within a passing period of time. For instance, everybody has developed the particularities of his or her ideal person, and we can mislay these particularities to another person through illusion because physical apperance may be deceitful. This is why most times we do not succeed in trial RR, (which is a romantic relationship initiated without friendship first), however, until we find out the person possesing the expected particularities we will not enjoy a happy RR.

How to identify Illusion-induced RR

To identify an illusion-induced RR, take the following steps:

1. Go through the particularities list of your ideal person,

2. compare them by evaluating that of your present partner,

3. check if the missing gap (or qualities) can be filled,

4. if they can, then work out the modalities, but if they (it) cannot, in the case of not-marriage, quit the RR. However, it is marriage, pray or meet counselor.

Nevertheless, if you are emotional, the steps may be very difficult to perform because our subconscious mind is inarticulate in commnicating our feelings to the part of our conscious mind, thus you may remain unhappy. However, this does not totally deprive you from doing anything. You can first, *(if possible using the dominant concept of the law of subconscious mind)* delete the entire love scenes, and particularity created and stored in your subconsious mind, then through the outcomes of the *relationship force*, you can now proceed with the above outlined steps. Note that,

> *A relationship force is a free interaction of two behavioural patterns in an existing relationship. In this, a behavioural pattern refers to articulated attitude of each person towards the affected person. For instance, I have a behavioural pattern, and you too as well have a behavioural pattern. If we agreed into a RR, the interaction between our behavioural patterns will establish relationship forces, which will be producing the outcomes of our RR. It is these forces that dictate what happen, such as how peaceful we stay, care to each other, and so on and on in our RR.[17]*

---

17. I derived the expression from the economic term of market forces; which is an interaction between demand and supply. In other words, it is a derivative of economic market forces.

Model-induced

The word 'Model' is personally used term of referring to an 'ideal person'. Meeting an ideal person can easily lead to RR. Who is your ideal person? It is a person whose personality fits into your desiring particularity. This person fits in with most, if not all, of your preferrences in a life partner, i.e., future, vision, belief and value system, etc. In this case, the particularity of this person have been developed within you as a thought, then to feeling, which is mixed with emotion and, finally manifest physically at a meeting point. Once both of you meet, there will be a magnetic force (aura[18]) to stimulate each person attraction.

A significant character of a *model-induced* RR is that it can start in two different forms. For instance, it can emanate via freindship (a period of acquitance) or instantaneous (trial RR since they are not perfect sure for each other). This depends on the information stored in each person's subconscious mind, or from the effectiveness of the aura, but, the former is preferable and it is uncommon.

Unlike *illusion-induced*, RR induced by meeting the ideal person can always last long. It normarly lead to marriage because both persons share comon personalities, and accept each other's particularities. Its *situations elasticity of stability*[19] (i.e. its responsiveness of change in stability due to change in situations of things) is nearest to result. This signifies that this kind of RR is prone to stability, and that both persons can manage themselves out of any relationship crises or situations.

From the foregoing, model-induced is the desiring RR of every individual, although it is rare to be found. People, who are into it, wish to remain, and hate intruders. For a man, the best period in life to find an ideal woman is when life has not come to "rosy". This is a period of examination, and that of decision making for a life partner. However, this does not negate the possibility of finding an ideal person at affluence period of life.

---

18. Aura is a paranormal force emanating from somebody or something: a force that is said to surround all people and objects, discernible, often as a bright glow, only to people of unusual psychic sensitivity. (Microsoft® Encarta® 2009. © 1993-2008 Microsoft Corporation. All rights reserved.)
19. Change in RR stability due to change in situations in which the RR is existing.

For a woman, it may be better to resist the influence of money around you. This is because money can influence the outcome of the relationship force, and it will produce false outcomes. Thus, this will therefore pass wrong information on your subconscious mind. This information will be under emotional control, and will always affect your relationship decision-making power.

How to track an Ideal Person

The personality of every individual is in two groups; the intrinsic and extrinsic parts. The intrinsic part consist of innate (or inborn) characteristics of a person, for example, natural appearance, innate sense of style, way of speaking, intonation, et cetera. In other hand, the extrinsic part are of those characteristics, for example, quality of western education acquired, values and belief system due to institutional upbringing, mode of dressing, affluence level, family background, et cetera.

In the search of an ideal person, I suggest that preference should be given to anyone who has your desired intrinsic values. This is because most of the intrinsic values are not easy to develop, since they are natural. You can guide somebody to develop almost all the extrinsic values, but not that of the intrinsic values.

Need-induced

> *The way lubricant makes an engine to run smoothly without crack, so as money makes a Love Relationship (LR) also to run smoothly without crack. Therefore, money is a lubricant, which makes LR to run smoothly wihout sharp noise.*

I personally use the word "need" as a generic term for material things. This includes need for money, sex, comfort, protection, affluence life, marriage, et cetera. It is the primary cause of every RR, and the bedrock in which every other forms of RR are built upon.

The natural desire in everyone to satisfy his or her need always induce people into RR. For instance, for a man and woman to sign-on a RR both have their latent needs back on their minds. That is to say, a man does not just sign up a woman for RR simple because he needs the presence of a woman, likewise a woman. There is always the presence of latent-needs, which may not be in negotiation, or observed, but secretly considered as a thought in each person.

> *My mum told me that the latent-needs of a man in any RR are sex, marriage or both. For a woman, they are protection, money, marriage, sex, or all.*

The above statement is common among blacks, especially the Sub-saharan region where folkway has traditionalised man to be the material provider, such as money for clothing, skin caring, shopping spree, et cetera in every RR, while the woman may recompense with her body for the man in sexual need[20].

However, this does not negate the existence of gigolo practices, and as well does not disprove the fact in some occasion where most good and innocent women have been catering for their men and at the sametime keep their body for them. The truth is that such women have made up their mind for marriage.

For stability, RR induced by 'Need' may last or not, depending on the 'intent' of its establishment. Its *conditions elasticity of stability* (i.e its responsiveness of change in stability due to change in conditions of things), varies according to the provision capacity of the man, and sometimes the expected responsiveness of the woman in particular.

---

20. The observation is only by exprience, and without any scientific research.

Nevertheless, in the middle of its existence, it can transmute into model or illusion induced. For model induced, the partners may come to understand that they have each other's particularities and will decide to progress as there may be a change of course. In the other hand, if it is illusion-induced, they may reach to break up point only if the "needs" that is serving as the stilt of the relationship is no longer visible.

> *During my undergraduate years, I have a neighbour who graduated, but, has no white-collar job and was living with his girl friend. He supported the girl in every form to realize her graduation, but, later was jilted after the girl defended her final year project. The stilt of the relationship was pulled down, when she realised that there is no need of staying with him again; first, she cannot marry him, secondly, she is true with her study, and she pulled down the stilt. It was a painful experience.*

The woman acted that way because her needs were realised, and there was no other bond to drive the relationship forward. However, that is often the case when LR (Love Relationship) lacks attachment. It is attachment, which has the emotional bond to drive LR into marriage. We will learn about that later.

SOME LATENT CIRCUMSTANCE OF NEED-INDUCED

Beware of nibble RR. In a nibble RR, either both persons, or one of them just wants to satisfy his or her need, thus quit the RR. Take for instance, where a boy walks into a girl's life, spend money for her, 'laid' her, and felt to dump her. This is dangerous because the 'dumping' may not be too easy.

Latent circumstances of need-induced are some unexpected experiences we observe in ongoing RR. They are latent because we never envisage or envision their occurrences. Although, people are experiencing them, but few has taken notice of the paranormal force behind their occurrence. For instance, lets look into some circumstances whereby sometimes people accept unwanted RR, remain in unhappy RR, or glued in a RR they wanted to nibble and run away. The instances include:

- *A case where a man's initial course for a woman is only for sexual interest, but as time progressed, he gets trapped, thus glued to unwanted RR. In most case got married to the woman.*

- *The same to a woman whose initial interest is to rip a man off, but with time, she gets hooked into the unwanted RR, and perhaps married the man, who is never the expected person.*

The question remains, what force is behind it? It is a paranormal force, emanating from relationship force and subconscious mind. The mystery of the occurrence can be attributed to this saying, *"familiarity breeds likeness and as well hatred."* It can even lead to sexual indulgence, thus develop any kind of Love Relationship.

Just as we can analyse the life of an organization with SWOT (Strength, Weakness, Opportunity, and Threat) Analysis, we can in the same manner agree on existence of the Personality SWOT Analysis (PSA) of people in their relationship. Take for instance, somebody you do not like may utilize the closeness opportunity made available, thus use his strength as a decoy to change you from your initial course towards him, then put on back the initial interest once you are trapped.

How is it possible? Just remember how your conscious mind conveys information to the subconscious mind during your *alpha state*. Relationship force can establish images as thoughts into your subconscious mind through your sensory perception especially as the circumstance is visual, and these thoughts been settled in your mind, may strongly in terms of decision-making be overriding the logic parts of your brain, thus be stimulating you to behave in the way you always regret or never intend to behave. Take for instance, sometimes you may no longer have interest to remain in a particular relationship, but you find it hard to quit, even as you are not happy in such relationship.[21]

The truth is that your subconscious mind often overpowers your conscious mind in decision-making relatively to the situation. The conscious mind through the logic part of your brain will make the rightful decision, but because the decision is not in harmony with that of the subconscious mind, you will lack willpower to carryout the decision. Take note of this state below, which we have explained in the last chapter:

> ...*the conscious mind has the "**Will**" and the subconscious mind has the "**Power**". When the conscious mind and subconscious mind are in harmony, you have "willpower", and become a "single-minded person". But, when they are in conflict, there is no willpower, and you become are a "double-minded" person.*[22]

---

21. So I am asking, you do not like a person, why given a chance. This is a risk worth not taking. Always adopt Refusal Skill, and not Negotiation Skill.
22. It is quoted from page 43 of the book; "The Power of Your Subconscious Mind" written by Harry W. Carpenter.

CRITERIA FOR ESTABLISHING LOVE RELATIONSHIP

In establishing or building a love relationship (LR), there is always the need to develop criteria in which the relationship should operate. The greatest challenge of our present day LR is lack of criteria. Many people are ignorance of this need, thus they respond with overwhelming of feelings in any relationship they found themselves.

LR is not centred only on "the way we feel", but it is all about 'Principles' and 'Boundaries'. It is issue of life and death, therefore requires carefulness before establishment. For a LR to achieve its purpose of establishment, it must have an important underlying ways it works, and these ways must exist as principles that govern it. Moreover, when it has not transmuted into marriage affair, it must have limits, base on the way some certain actions should be exhibits, and these limits should be acknowledged as boundaries cum principles of the relationship actions.

The Principle of Tre-aars-flukt

As we state above, it is necessary for a Love Relationship (LR) to have principles in which it is been established. Our principle in this point is the *Principle of Tre-aars-flukt*[23], which constitutes eight different principles. They are *reciprocity, respect, responsibility, forgiveness, labour, understanding, care, and tolerance*. These principles must serve as the bedrock and framework of every LR, whether in marriage or RR. For result, when properly practised, their attribution will lead every relationship to achieve the expected dream.

Reciprocity: This principle is the major determinant of a relationship or friendship, and once it does not exist, it means there is no existing relationship or friendship. This is because it expresses the practice of mutual exchange, especially of giving respect, regard, and caring in return. Therefore, in every relationship there must be existence of reciprocity of caring, respect, and regard between the persons. Although, this may not be in perfect equivalent, but must be noticed with impact.

---

23. I personally developed this principles, and its pronounciation is framed from 3Rs (RRR)-FLUCT.

Respect: This principle expresses the practice of respect. There must be a mutual exchange of respect, i.e., respect-returned for respect-received. To respect in this aspect means to hold each other in a high esteem, honour and treat each other as worthwhile, even when you are more privileged than the other person is. In addition, the respect must be in extension of each other's background, meaning that we must respect each other background.

Responsibility: For this principle, there must be a sharing of responsibilities. This indicates that both should depend on each other, i.e. a man should carry the woman's responsibilities as well as the woman carries that of the man, although for some extent.

Forgiveness: There must be an act of pardoning each other's mistakes or wrongdoings when the need arises. No relationship can exist without forgiveness. To forgive is beyond to-forget. In real practice, forgiveness involves that we will no longer dwell on that person's mistakes, use the mistake against the person, and relate it (the mistake) to a third party.

Labour: This principle states that both persons must labour for the smooth workability and stability of the relationship. To labour means to work hard, and put much effort into the establishment and stability of the relationship. Although, one person can still labour for the establishment of a relationship, but its stability and longitivity are at stake.

Understanding: This recommends the existing of understanding between both. To understand means to be knowledgeable about each other's personality SWOT. For feeling improvement, it is necessary to know each other's daily activities.

Caring: For this principle, there must be a mutual exchange of caring for each other, i.e. caring-returned for caring-received. But, sex must not be practised the way it is explained in "need-induced relationship." For instance, the woman must not use sex (or her body) for a recompense. It must be a normal exercise in existence, and as both are liable to protect, provide for, or pay attention, and feeling of love for each other. In addition, caring to know each other's list-to-do every day is a strong tool.

Tolerance: For this principle, there must be a high level of tolerance of each other's weaknesses. For effectiveness, the best way to apply this principle is to run a Personality SWOT Analysis (PSA) of your partner. The analytical process should achieve the followings:

- *Understanding of the* **strengths** *of your partner, which should be a key focus. By identifying them, it will help you support the person to build his or her attitude towards perfection.*

- *The* **weaknesses** *have to be observe, and must be follow up with a moderate tolerance.*

- *It will be good to understand the available* **opportunities** *in the person's life, as it will help the person's future development.*

- *It is good to expose the* **threats** *that might hamper the relationship in future. A good example of such threat is lost-love. Most people's lost–love can be haunting their present relationship, in other words, the existence of a past lover may be a threat to the new lover.*

Overview of the Principles

From the upshot of the above principles, *understanding, tolerance, reciprocity,* and *forgiveness* are the major bedrock of every relationship. But, the principle of Tolerance does not support the practice of unlimited tolerance (this is impossible), rather it only accept moderate tolerance.

Reciprocity in the other hand, does not support uncaring, disrespect, and disregard returns. Likewise the Responsibility principle, which does not mandate equal responsibility distributions and, Forgiveness, which also does not support repetitive mistakes, and constant demand for forgiveness.

The truth is that we can hardly find a relationship where all these principles are working perfectly, even in a harmonized marriage.

BOUNDARIES TO SET IN ANY RELATIONSHIP

To prevent a cog in the wheel of progress, the wheel of progress must be grease with a lubricant. That is to say, the *principle of tre-aars-flukt* will work smoothly and effectively only if a relationship constitutes, and maintains some boundaries. Below are some boundaries of a relationship:

- Both have to agree if there may be sexual indulgence,
- They must agreed, if anybody can have extra affair, whether casual or strong,
- Agreed on what should be expected from each other,
- They must establish the basic "do-and-don't" of each other,
- Agreed, if the relationship should be an open or closed type. An open relationship is made known to the public, while close relationship will be existing in secret.
- There must be an agreement on the 'intent' of the relationship, such intent must be in this three conditions:

    1. *Marriage interest is of possibility-based,*
    2. *Marriage interest is of probability-based,*
    3. *Just for sex and other motives excluding marriage.*

Generally, in every relationship, due to the existence of relationship force relatively to the subconscious and conscious mind, sometimes our expected experience may be different from our observed experience, therefore relationship boundaries can be reset or adjusted. In addition, most of the boundaries are basic and should be established during negotiation, while some are set when the relationship is in progress.

TYPES OF RELATIONSHIP

There is a difference between "cause-and-effect". The forms of relationship have explained the three stimulating factors as the causes of relationship. Remember that these factors are illusion, model, and need as we stated earlier. Now the type of relationship is to teach the effect of relationship. However, some writers in different terms may have outlined various types of relationship[24], however, this is quite different from that of this work as they are been derived from my observed trend of relationships, thus I personally named them *survival, positive, negative,* and *compensatory* type of relationships.

Survival Relationship

This is a relationship where one person is a Parasite and the other a Provider[25]. The Parasite lives and survived on the Provider. The relationship is on a course of good path so long as its *provisional function*[26] is constant.

Here, the application of the reciprocity principle is base on the mutual exchange of sex and material (or physical) things, and the relationship intent often exists in two conditions.

For the first condition, if the woman is a Parasite, it is either she accepts the man (who stands like the Provider), marries her due to what she is benefiting, or she quits after sometime. In the other hand, if the man is the Parasite, either it is for sexual or marriage motives, otherwise he may likely quit. To show love, it is rare for the woman love the man, and the man may be expose to the danger of heartbreak.

In the second condition, if the woman is a Provider, she may be committed for marriage and less in sexual activities, unless in the case of gigolo, where the situation may be more of sexual drive than marriage interest. Although, there may be an exceptional case, where both marriage and sexual activity may be the intent drivers. But, like that of the initial condition, the Provider is also exposes to the danger of heartbreak, and at a higher risk.

---

24. Although, I have not come across such in any article or book,
25. By parasite, I am referring to a person whose economic sustenance depends on another person's provision.
    And provider; a person that to cater for the parasite.
26. the functional relationship between a LR and its depending factors.

Furthermore, for marriage propositions considering the first condition, the probability of the Parasite marrying the Provider is very high, or close to one. This is because majority of women by nature use provisions capacity as a key determinant factor of choosing a man. That is to say, a woman can marry a man if he is capable of meeting her material needs.

However, in the second condition, it may be difficult for the man as a Parasite to marry the woman (who is the provider). This is because first, no man wants to accept his parasitic state in a marriage, except few weak economic men. Secondly, men want to remain the head, and thirdly, when a woman input so much of her value (e.g. the value of her body), and wealth in a relationship, then like commodity that is supposed to produce additional satisfaction to the man in a later time of the marriage, she may lose her initial value.

Although, the reason behind this third point, is the psychological effect of human nature, whereby we give less regard to the things of abundancy, and more desire and value to the things of scarcity, ceteris paribus. Therefore, the *additional satisfaction* the man supposed to derive from marrying her may reduce. Meaning that to the man, nothing is new about the woman. Nevertheless, there is exceptional cases where the man in his parasitic state may marry the woman, but depending on the form of attachment existing between them. The danger is that if the woman is not a prudent type, such offer may cost the man his family headship.

For effect, the existence of a Parasite and Provider signifies this type of relationship (i.e. survival relationship) to be 'need-induced effect'. Therefore for suggestions:

> *If a man is a Provider, he should spend judiciously to the woman and lay not much hope on her.*

> *For the woman as a Provider, the suggestion is the same like that of the man, except, she should stop sexual indulgence with the man.*

To a high extent, the driving force of a survival relationship is material provision, except in a situation where the Provider has a strong sexual power. Although, the Parasite may still leave, if there is no (or a short fall in the) material supply, therefore a Provider must play with his or her conscious mind rather than emotion.

Positive Relationship

Two persons are into a positive relationship only if, a rise in the feeling of care of one-person leads to the rise in that of the affected person feeling of care. In other words, there is no disticnt Provider or Parasite as each person can depend and provide for each other.

A positive relationship naturally exists in the subconscious mind of the actors, and its principle driving force is that of understanding, tolerance, forgiveness, and reciprocity.

Although, it is not common, but it is in existence, and the affected persons share the same desiring particularities before meeting each other. They care for each other, always feel happy when being together, and unhappy when missing each other.

Generally, such relationship has longevity advantage, but separation is disastrous. People that experienced this type of relationship, and later due to any reason got breakup, may hardly take their next relationship serious, although there are exceptional cases. From our expressions so far, this might be part of the reasons while sometimes a person may not be putting much effort in her or his present relationship due to a breakup exprience of the previous positive relationship. Lastly, positive-relationship is an effect of model-induced form of relationship.

Negative Relationship

This type of relationship exists between *Uninterested* and *Interested* persons. The term 'Uninterested' is referring to a person who is not putting much effort for the growing of his or her relationship, and 'Interested' for the person who is putting a greater efforts. Here, an *interested person (IP)* may serve as a parasite (on sexual bases) or a provider (for both sex and material provisions). The *uninterested person (UP)* may have no feeling of care for the IP whose needs may be sex, marriage, material, or all.

For development, the driving force of the relationship is 'persuasion', which will mostly be an outcome from the IP.

In gender perspective, if the IP is a man, his intents may be sex, marriage, material things, or all. If it is a woman, the case is the same, but with higher degree on marriage interest. Empirically, women who provide sex and other needs to men are for marriage, unless in the condition of gigolo.

However, for uninterested persons, a man may be UP because the woman is not the ideal person or he is under overwhelming influence. In the other hand, for a woman, it may be the man's provision incapablity or also under overwhelming influence. But, there are exceptional cases where a woman plays along with hidden interest, just with reason of sizing the man's interest.

For sexual indulgence, if the UP is a woman, her sexual activites with the man may be rare. If the man on the other hand is UP, he may hardly care materially for the woman, but may highly indulge into sex with the woman depending on attractiveness status of the woman. Therefore, there is a probability that a man will pay much, and sleep much with a woman, but will not have a significant interest on that woman.

Generally, negative-relationship is highly associated with an ending part of broken relationship, and it is an effect of *need-induced* or *illusion-induced* relationship. From the above expressions, one party may be nagging, and even if it leads to marriage, it may not be strong.

> *Negative relationship does not worth practicing. This is because when a person is forcing himself or herself into a relationship, the person is looking for violence.*

Compensatory Relationship

Compensatory tendency can push a person into a relationship. For example, they said, "pity is akin to love." It is empirical to say that pity has led some people into relationships. For example, I have seen a case where a man after explaining a particular ordeal to a woman, then was pitied by the woman, therefore from pity to love, although, the relationship did not lead to marriage.[27]

However, not only pity, what about conformity, most people at their early teens invlove into relationship due to conformity. So this type of relationship exists due to some compensatory factors. It is like a positive relationship, but without a definite long-term objective.

> *I remembered during my undergraduate years when most of our female folks compensated their male folks in relationship for the sake of academic work supports. Although, most of these relationships ended after we left school.*

---

27. That was during my university undergraduate days in 2001 to 2005.

For factor or form inducement, compensatory relationship by nature is of hybrid-induced. It is connected with model-induced, and need-induced. For the model-induced, the Provider accepts the Parasite due to some of his or her particularities, while for the need-induced, the UP may accept the IP in order to show appreciation, or illustrate rewardness.

For principles of establishment, *reciprocity, understanding, labour,* together with other principles are often effective, and this may be due to influence of *"I am serious."* Although, many of them do not last to the point of marriage, but we can still ask such question like:

"Why does compensatory relationship in many cases not lead to marriage?"

I have had a deep thought on the reasons why it rarely leads to marriage. A love relationship is mark for an achievement, if it finally led to marriage, and any of them that fail this test did not last.

On why it rarely leads to marriage is that such relationship always come to an end once the compensatory goal is achieved. Take for instance, *in my undergraduate years experience, which I mentioned above,* most of the RR ended as soon as we left school. However, there is an exceptional case where it can lead to marriage. For instance, if a compensatory relationship that ended some years comes back, and reunioned, there is a nearer possibility of marriage. How is it possible?

If two people who had been in compensatory relationship missed each other for some period of years, and later meet again, if both of them re-establish their relationship, there is a higher degree of marriage. This is because the existed gap between them may in different occasions created rooms for the reflection of the past as thoughts and feelings. It is during these times that the whole experience of the past may be downloaded into each person's subconscious mind, and once both of them meet for a second time, the psychological effect of missing each other for sometimes may prompt the desire to have each other again.

Like we mentioned above, the reason behind this psychological effect is our human nature of giving less regard to the things of abundancy, and more desiring and higher value to the things of scarcity or things we have missed for sometimes, ceteris paribus. Supportively, relatively to our previous chapter learning, once the previous love-enjoyed experience are transferred into the subsconscious mind of the affected persons, separation may be difficult, unless via the process of deletion, or reprogramming of the subconscious mind with the necessary laws of the subconscious mind and, which may take time to perform.

THE KEY BUILDERS OF RELATIONSHIP

Sex and time is the distinct builder of LR. To some people (i.e. sex believers), sex indulgence is the signatory to commence every relationship, while some (i.e. time believers) believed that familiarity based on time would breed likeness, thus lead to sex, which may lead to LR.

The viewpoint of Sex believers

To widen the argument, those arguing for sexual indulgence are on the viewpoint that the pressing and primary motive of a man to a woman for a relationship is sex. They believed that an instant sexual intercourse with a woman is the only way to forceful commit her into a relationship. To them, a woman will only accept and respect a man when sexual activity might have taken place between both of them, therefore sexual intercourse is a necessary condition, and all other conditions are for sufficient reasons.

The viewpoint of Time believers

However, the second set of people believed on time factor. To them, relationship as a function of time enables the affected persons period of time to create a room for acquaintance, thus transmute the friendship into a strong relationship, which will later turn into RR. So time for understanding each other is the most necessary condition, and all other conditions including sex are for sufficient condition, but not necessary.

The hybrid viewpoint

Although, I have taken time to examine the two viewpoints and accept the fact that both are in the same domain. The truth is that both adoption of time or sex factor as a preferred strategy depends on the woman existing as approachable-woman. Every woman has a different mode of responding to a man in terms of friendship and relationship.

For time adoption, some women prefer men within a time frame, and their initial motive is acquitance. These set of women believed sexual activity to be for sufficient condition, but not necessary in the early time of a relationship. So they will first love a man before sexual commitment. In addition, they give time a chance in order to observe the man's particularity, and will allow the particularity to settle in their heart as thought before they will commit themselves.

For sexual adoption, if a man's approach is not sexually in direction, most women may not take such man serious. For instance some of these women, when close with them no matter the size of your kindness to them, if you made no sexual move or request within a time, in eventuality of a departure, they may easily forget you. But, there is exceptional case where some of them see you as a 'big brother'. In addition, they often, love a man after sex. It is after this period that they will allow the particularity of the man to settle in their heart. Therefore, by examining women based on these differents psychological states of responsiveness approach, I grouped them into three[28], which are the *fox, dog,* and the *sheep.*

The Fox

They are those women no matter how close a man is to them, if there is no sexual involvement, they will not develop any feeling of love for the man. Sometimes with sexual involvement, yet they may still develop no feeling for the opposite sex. They see their body as a valuable asset. To them sex indulgence signifies commitment in a relationship. They are need consciousness and may only fall for a man based on his provision capacity.

When you meet a fox, she looks very cunnying and crafty in getting her needs from men. Because of their material consciousness, they often give chance to nearly every man that comes on their ways. They are seductive and exploitative with manipulation in dealings. Most of them are with a lot of sex appeal because that is their means of creating attention from men. Some of them are initial givers of gifts, and can respond in pretence of being in love with initial gift provision at the early stage, but this is a bait. In response, most men normally failed short to observe this initial gift as bait by accepting the gift they open up their subconscious mind to be storing more coming of what might look like love scenes, and may be trap in the game.

Among the major characters of a fox, she keeps her body for men who have the capable to provide most of her needs. However, not all fox can keep different men at the sametime. Most of them (for attachmend reason) can keep a single man and still relate to other men in their foxy way of life.

---

28. I coined the terms; dog, sheep, and fox base on the behaviour of the relative animals.

For Personality SWOT Analysis (PSA), the *strength* of a fox lies on her emotionless state in some relationship, and the respect she attaches to her body, although her body may go for material exchange, but not all forms of exchange. Thanks to her willpower. Their major *weakness* is greed. They place their priority on the material benefits they may get from a man, and most of them are very expensive. For their *opportunity*, if a fox attached emotion in a relationship she will last long, so long as her demands are satisfied, and for her *threat*, they are crafty, cunning with exploitation and manipulation in nature.

Generally, it is dangerous relating with a fox with emotional mindset, their relationship is a game of wit, and it often exists in need-induced relationship.

Although, I guess you may ask a question on how to identify a fox. There is no general way to identify a fox because women are indefinable, but as a man, in pretence make a predatory sexual advance against her, watch her response, and at the sometime, they are material conscious.

However, there is existence of *fox men*. In a brief discussion, despite how women may be close to them, and they will hardly develop feeling for them. In every relationship, they work with their conscious mind (less emotional state). To them, sex is a key factor that keeps them in a relationship. They can spend much just to have a sex with a desired woman.

For PSA, their *strength* is on their consciousness mindset, thus making them to be less emotional like their opposite (fox women). Their *weakness* is much of sexual desire, and it irritates them when a woman do not give them a chance to expolit their body. For one part of their *opportunity*, if they eventually love a woman, then can keep that woman, although this will not stop them from other women, and as their *threat*, are also like that of their female.

The Dog

Have you seen women who strongly desire sexually for any kind of men that get close to them? Yes. Such women exist. To them, to love is to sex. The fundamental cause may be of biological reactions (i.e. the nature of their reproductive system), peer induced pressure, fornication or adulterous spirit[29], etc., which is out of our scope. They are on course for sexual reason in every relationship involved. In addition, to some of them, the reasons might include material need, or it is their life style. While to some, a little gift gets them off. They possess the attitude of shamelessness, this is because they can have it (sex) with you, your brother, and friends, and do not last in a relationship.

---

29. For those who believed in such spirit.

Moreover, when you meet a dog, she looks very seductive. What keeps both of you going is her sexual drive. Get a good setting and get in with her, she will have it with you. She is not expensive and a dip ditch.

For PSA, her seductive power can be *strength* to her, although may be regard as a *weakness* by men around her. Since she may be less expensive, this is also a *weakness* to her and *opportunity* for her 'suckers'. Lastly, her unfaithfulness character is a *threat* to any man that wants to marry her.

How can a person identify a dog? She is a seducer, but you must be very careful not to confuse her with a fox. This is because most fox use seduction as bait against men, especially the men they want to rip off.

Secondly, in pretence take a predatory sexual move against that person, and carefully observe her response. It will be good, if we do not fall in love or keep a relationship with a dog, and even the dog men are like the women. They have only one aim, which is sex indulgence.

The Sheep (female and male)

The sheep believed that sex indulgence in a relationship is not a necessary condition, but a sufficient condition. To them, a good relationship must involve the passing of two different stages before its attainment. These stages include first, friendship, and secondly, intimacy less sex.

Therefore, they believed that familiarity through acquaintance breeds love. They have the intuitive knowledge that friendship creates room for learning and acquaintance with each other. In their believe, this process continually may lead to intimacy (much closeness less sex), then finally, if it continues, it will lead to relationship, and all these must be within a period of time. This is why they a time believers.

For PSA, among their *strength* are observation skill and ability to rate the particularities of their friends in the period of friendship. The observation skill helps them to learn their partners' personalities, as they relate within their conscious mind at the friendship state. Another of their character is their undying love tendency. This might look like a *weakness* or *strength* because they love with their subconscious mind. Although, despite it often takes time for them to fall in love, but once they are in, they normally last long. Their *opportunity* is hope of marriage, which they give their partners. For *threat*, it is always good not to have long lasting problem with them, as it may takes time to win them back.

The sheeps are everyone ideal kind of persons. They are trust worthy, responsible, and focus in relationship, but they are not common to have.

General Classification

For the sake we are dynamic human beings, the Sheep, Fox, and Dog are kinds of quality of mind of different persons as we learnt above. In other ways, they are responsive-love relationship life styles of people. However, as a type of trait (or temperament), nobody is definite of any of them in nature. That is to say, the fact that a person for instance is a fox in a particular relationship does not mean that the person cannot be a sheep in another relationship. Although, this depends on whom the person meets. Some persons can be a sheep in a particular relationship due to motive, and as well be a fox in another relationship due to another motive.

Nevertheless, if we refer someone as a sheep, we are talkng about the mood that possesses the highest frequency in various relationship experiences of the person. For instance, if the dominant mood in your relationship is a foxy way of life style, that means you are a fox.

LIFE CYCLE OF AN UNBREAKABLE RELATIONSHIP

Unbreakable relationship exists when an existing relationship never runs into an end irrespective of all experienced conditions or situations, except dead. An example is marriage, according to God's ordination. Following this, every love relationship is characterised by series of phases that are self-repeating in a circular manner.

There are three phases in a love relationship (especially that of marriage), which permanently repeat in a circular manner within a period of time. Base on their characters, these phases are termed as *Nova, Sombre,* and *Ebb*.[30]

Among these phases, none of them stays permenantly in its state. This is because the relationship force functions to change them in different periods, due to this, what emantes as relationship observations or outcomes from the relationship forces to the mind varies. This is why sometimes we face the nova, later the sombre, and then the ebb phase repeating in a circular mannner.

The below diagram dipicts the movement cycle of a relationship from nova to sombre, sombre to ebb, and ebb to nova, all in a circular manner.

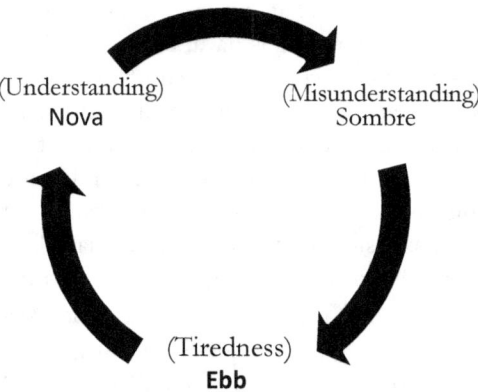

(Understanding)
Nova

(Misunderstanding)
Sombre

(Tiredness)
Ebb

---

30.   I noticed that there are three phases in a love relationship (especially that of marriage), which permanently repeat in a circular manner within a period of time. Personally I termed these phases as Nova, Sombre, and Ebb.

The Nova Phase

The word 'nova' is derived from the terminology of astronomers. It means a star, whose brightness suddenly gets exploded, but did not last long, and in this book, it is used as a short pleasant period in a love relationship.

The beginning of every love relationship is like a nova. It has a sudden bright phase that does not last. How? At the *nova phase* of a relationship, both persons enjoy the happiness of the union. The responsible causes include the fresh and high desire of each other. Each person responds with a strong caring attitude as the strong passion of love drives their togetherness smoothly. However, following the Heraclitus philosophy[31] of *"all is flux"*, the nova phase with its sudden brightness must get dark. Though, no condition is unmangeable, so they can still call each other to order. Neverthelsess, no matter what care, and efffort they may put, the phase of sombre (a short period of unpleasant period in a relationship) is inevitable. So they will misunderstand each other, and probably get quarrel.

The force behind the effect of the relationship to move from nova to sombre phase is what we need to know. Obviously, misunderstanding is an effect and not the cause. That is to say, the movement as a change is natural, and misunderstanding as well is natural.

In every relationship, the ocurrence of quarrel is a natural phenemenon. That is to say, quarreling is natural, and normal. In the positive side, it is good because it has a latent advantage of creating understanding out of dissension. Take for instance, we all have similar and dfferent human traits, if two people are close friends, thus establish a relationship, there is a possibility of dissension that can lead to quarrel. This is because of their behavioural or role conflicts *(a struggle for dominance by two different behavioural pattern)*, that is to say, the free interaction between their similarities will create understanding, thus a happy and enjoyable moments. In the other hand, that of the differences will create dissension, thus unhappy moments. Therefore, the outcome of the relationship force depends on the interactive flow of the two persons' similarities, and their differences. Like we have mentioned before, for the similarities, it is issue of understanding, and for the differences, it is the works of misunderstanding. It is this circumstance, and conditions of the misunderstanding that will dim the nova phase of the relationship, thus occasion it into sombre, which can be call Sombre (dark and gloomy) occasion.

---

31. Heraclitus of Ephesus (ca. 535 – 475 BC) was a pre-Socratic Greek philosopher, a native of Ephesus, Ionia, on the coast of Asia Minor. He is famous for his doctrine of change being central to the universe. His famous sayings, "All is flux", and "You cannot step twice into the same river" is still remembered today.

The Sombre Phase

As mentioned above, this phase is characterised with inevitable unpleasant period that will not last long. The two persons or lovers will experience misunderstanding, probably fight in some situations. But, because the phase cannot stay permanently, through the relationship force, there will be a move for a new phase, which will be expected to cause a change in the relationship. This new phase will emerge as soon as the sombre phase touches its climax. In other words, the existing sombre phase must reach a climax because two lovers quarreling must be tired, and desire for peace, and the relationship will take a new phase, which is call ebb occasions.

The Ebb Phase

As the name implies, this phase exists to ebb away the dark phase of the Sombre. So, at the ending condition of the sombre, the two lovers will get tired, thus through the prevailing relationship force, the need to have anew phase will surface. But, by which instrument? By the instrument of any of the principle of tre-aars-flukt, and boundaries of LR through which the relationship was established, and in which there shall be a check on them. Then adjustment will take place, and peace, happiness and enjoyable moment will resurface, thus the nova phase will be re-establish, so the process continues one after the other, running in a circular manner.

Benefits of the Phases

The above-explained phases have their different stages benefits they fashioned in a love relationship. The benefits of the nova phase exposes us to the experience of pleasant moment. The sombre creates the opportunity for us to observe and understand each person's weakness, and the ebb phase helps us to amend our differences.

Assumption of the Concept

The concept of life cycle of unbreakable relationship is explained with the assumption where a relationship is unbreakable except in the subject of death.

THE COMPOSITION OF LOVE RELATIONSHIP

So far, in this learning, the term *Love Relationship (LR)* has been in connotation with marriage and *Romantic Relationship (RR)*. In this issue, the compositional stages are the stages in which a LR is established and exists. In other words, they are the driving forces existing as theatrical stages in an ongoing LR. Take for instance, in a LR, we experience passion for mating (sexual desire), and physical admiration, which can lead us into love arena, thus RR. Moreover, we can also experience passsion for mating, physical admiration, and emotional bond for togetherness, which can lead us into marriage.

For impact, it is the structural forces of LR, which determine the survival of every LR. They are structural to a LR because they are in stages. They are forces because they are invisible, but yeild physical results. Like mentioned above, they occur as stages, and determine how long a LR will last, and can be refer as stages of love.

Stages of Love

Some love experts like Helen Fisher (2004) and Winston Roberts (2004) wrote about them[32]. Helen divided the stages into three, namely: lust, attraction, and attachment. According to her:

> *"Lust makes people like each other, romantic attraction encourages people to focus on mating, and attachment helps people tolerate the spouse"* [33]

For more explanation, Winston Roberts (2004) stated:

> *"Lust is the initial passionate sexual desire that promotes mating, and involves the increased release of chemicals such as testosterone and estrogen. These effects rarely last more than a few weeks or months. Attraction is the more individualized and romantic desire for a specific candidate for mating, which develops out of lust as commitment to an individual mate forms. Recent studies in neuroscience have indicated that as people fall in love, the brain consistently releases a certain set of chemicals, including pheromones, dopamine, norepinephrine, and serotonin, which act in a manner similar to amphetamines, stimulating the brain's pleasure center and leading to side effects such as increased heart rate, loss of appetite and sleep, and an intense feeling of excitement. Research has indicated that this stage generally lasts from one and a half to three years."*

---

32. See **http://simple.wikipedia.org/wiki/Love**
33. See Helen Fisher (2004). Why We Love: The Nature and Chemistry of Romantic love. New York. Henry Holt and Company.

He continues,

> *"Since the lust and attraction stages are both considered temporary, a third stage is needed to account for long-term relationships. Attachment is the bonding that promotes relationships lasting for many years and even decades. Attachment is generally based on commitments such as marriage and children, or on mutual friendship based on things like shared interests. It has been linked to higher levels of the chemicals oxytocin and vasopressin to a greater degree than short-term relationships have."* [34]

In alignment with Fisher's work, in any ongoing LR between two people; the love pattern is subject to changes, that is to say, it constitutes dynamic movement from one stage to another within a period of time. The first stage is *lust*, followed by *attraction*, and *attachment* as the final stage. However, so long as the LR is in existence, none of these stages can phase off permanently, rather the dominant stage is assumed to be the LR stage. Take for instance, these condtions:

- *The current stage of a given LR is lust, if the tendency of lust is dominant and strong, attraction is weak and, perhaps exist but unnoticed, and attachment is weak, unnoticed or does not exist.*

- *The current stage of a given LR is attractive, if the tendency of attraction is dominant and strong, lust is weak, although noticeable, or exhausted, and attachment is weak, noticeable or does not exist.*

- *The current stage of a given LR is attachment, if the tendency of attachment is dominant and strong, lust is weak, perhaps exist but unnoticed, or exhausted, and attraction is weak, unnoticed or exhausted.*

---

34. Winston, Robert (2004). Human. Smithsonian Institution. ISBN 0-03-093780-9

The Drivers of the Stages

The stages of love, which are lust, attraction, and attachment remains the work of Helen Fisher, however, the stage drivers are the inclusion of my work as I explained in the preceding page.

In life, there are values, beliefs, interest, et cetera. In career or relationship issues of life, there are two set of people, *lover relationship conscious people,* and *career conscious people.* However, to everyone existing in the various stages of love of life, there is a driver or drivers serving as the force(s) pushing the person. Some people are being driven by lust, so they are *lust conscious people.* What brings them close into LR is sexual drive. If there is no strong attraction, or attachment binding them, most of them leave when this phase get weak, or exhausted. For instance, in the *love responsive approach*, which we learnt, majority of Dogs are lust conscious persons, while few of the Fox are also the same.

Moreover, in the case of attraction, some are *attractive conscious people.* The driver behind these people is *intrinsic values,* such as physical appearance. Take for instance, an attractive conscious person may often desired to see and stay around the attracted person not primarily because of mating, but because of likeness, although mating may be or not there. They normally stay even when the lust stage is weak or exhausted, and looking for other factors to stimulate the LR into the third stage. In the *love responsive approach* that we learnt, most Sheep, and few Foxes are the attractive conscious persons.

For the stage of attachment, the *attachment conscious people* are the emotional bond, and marriage conscious persons. They are being driven by the reasons of attachment, such as marriage. This is why they often talk about marriage in every LR they accepted. Some of the attachment values in this state are the *extrinsic values,* such as family background of the person, future of the person, social education status, the desires to have a child with such person due to some reasons, child rearing, etc. Those in this form of consciousness, once they are in LR, they are ready for marriage. In the *love responsive approach* that we learnt, most Sheep are the attachment conscious persons, and few Foxes whose marriage is their needs.

However, except in the form of career, and relationship consciousness, none of these other consciousness, such as lust, attraction, and attachment is static in state. All of them are dynamic consciousness, but what distinquish them is habit, traits, or addiction of love responsiveness life style of the actors. That is to say, nobody for instance is a *static lust conscious person*, the same to attraction, and attachment. All of us are dynamic beings, we change depending on the person we have as a partner. What really labels us is a question of habit, traits, or addiction. In this point, must people have the habit of lust, thus they are lust addicted, and the same to both of the attraction (attraction addicted), and attachment (attachment addicted).

From the foregoing, we can inductively explain the following statements:

- *Why your marriage is strong, or weak,*

- *Why your unmarried relationship is strong, or weak,*

Behind Attachment

As been stated early, it is the stage of atttachment that lead LR into marriage, and probably keep it flowing until when death do apart the involved persons, though this depend on the type and strength of the attachment. Moreover, an attachment also propels the changes that we just explained in the *Concept of Life Cycle of Unbreakable LR*. Take for instance, in the case of a married couple, it may be the forces that emanated from their past love experience, the sharing obligation to rear children (a child) toward greatness, or to achieve a particular vision as loved ones. It can be stronger, if the couple is attachment conscious individuals.

However, in a marriage where attachment is weak, such marriage may face progressive constraint. The constraint may emerge because of any of these followings:

- *One of them dwelling in the emotion of lost-love of the past,*

- *The marriage has no definite goal, or vision,*

- *Between the couple, one is lust active, and the other is indifferent as this may result to infidelity,* or

- *Any other not mentioned.*

Let us look into the last point, which stated;

"...that one is lust active, and the other is indifferent as this may result to infidelity."

For instance in a LR of young sexual active persons, say between WIF (the woman) and HUS (the man) , if WIF is still lust active to the HUS, and the HUS has reach his mating saturation point with her, meaning that every mating point between them may be forceful to HUS, but to the WIF, it may be sexual pleasure. This can lead the HUS into infidelity, which may be heading the marriage towards danger.[35]

One among the major reason why the HUS may 'cheat' or live under infidelity influence is because he no longer sexually desires the WIF, or his sexual desire towards the WIF is less strong. Perhaps they have mated much before they got married, and HUS had within that period, exhausted his passion for mating with her. He only accepted the marrage by attachment, and an example of such attachment may be the driven force of marriage promise, which may serve as the emotional bond that led him into the marriage.

To be precise in this point, and relatively to life experience, this is mostly the situation we found in marriage that exprienced so many years of RR, before it was finally established.

> *I have seen a marriage where husband can stay up to four months without touching his faithful wife, but often touch other women outside. Among my finding is that they were in RR for about twelve years before the marriage, and the prioritised attachment is marriage promise, and desire to have children together.*

Analyzing the case of my above experience, the LR of the marriage has lost its first and second stages, which are lust and attraction respectively, but was led into marriage by attachment. The woman (i.e. the wife) was the person carrying the higher degree of the emotional bond of the attachment. While the man (i.e. the husband), although bearing a less degree of the emotional bond of the attachment was influence by the driven force of marriage promise, which was the attachment.

---

35. Remember that indulging into sex with a person is a service, but service in the labour of love or labour of payment (as in the case of prostitution).

What is the lesson to learn from the marriage? So long as the psychological satisfaction state of human being exists, and except by the grace of God, the man is bind to infidelity. Although, he may be mating with his wife in some occasions, but such mating is for child bearing, which should not be the reason because sex in marriage has to be make, in order to lubricate the love feeling of the couple. If proper control is not been taking, the woman also beyond self-control can join the husband as an infidelity member, unless she wants to maintain her faithfulness. This situation in the life of the man can continue until when the man will reach his active sexual limit due to age or other factor.

However, to avoid this kind of experience, we need to live premarital undefile as been stated in the Scripture:

> *Marriage is honourable in all, and the bed undefiled: but whoremongers and adulterers God will judge. Hebrews 13:4*

The above bible quotation was not written only to fulfill righteousness or holiness, but also to help us avoid the experience of our lesson case. God who inspired his Saint in proclaiming such divine instruction saw all the danger of premarital defilement.

Behind Lust and Attraction

Lust and attraction first bring LR into a RR, before attachment finally will lead it into marriage. A RR is strong because both lust and attraction are active. However, it can be weak, if lust is exhausted, attraction is strong (or weak), and one of the partner is a relationship conscious person while the other is not. In this case, the RR may struggle for survival in order to meet the next stage. But, if both of them are relationship conscious persons, the LR may move into the third stage, which is attachment. Contrary, in a situation where both persons are not relationship conscious people, the RR may end.

Chapter Three

BEYOND THE CONTROLLING DRIVERS

Introduction

We have learnt most of the human psychological states that drive our loving pattern in love-relationship (LR). They are the psychological state that composed our nature of LR, and drive our responses and approaches. Most of them exist beyond our control, while some are within our control. To a reasonable state, by eliminating and including some techniques we struggle to fight them by trying to control ourselves no matter the intensity of our love feelings. However, it is unfortunate that most times, we cannot overcome them, therefore we relegate ourselves to them, and found ourselves being under their control, and takes order from them.

The truth is that human beings by nature like power, and always want to be in control. In LR, it is more pronounced in women that God has made to subordinate men. Therefore, in this chapter, we are to study the psychological states behind the person who is in control of an ongoing LR, and why you are not in control of your LR.

In every relationship between two people, the struggle of who shall be in control, thus the leading decision-maker is a common phenomenon. The thought of being in control is always hidden in the mind of the actors even before they began to love each other.

Naturally, human beings like to dominate, be in control, and have superiority over others. For when two people come close through relationship, there is a tendency of complex conflict between them. No one wants to be less important, and so for every LR, there is always a struggle of control over who may be taking majority of the decisions, therefore be in charge of the ongoing of the relationship. To a certain extent, it is true that this circumstance contributes to propel the *nova phase* into *sombre phase* as we discussed in our last chapter.

In the early stage of a relationship between two people, *"who to be in control"* exists as a hidden objective in each other's minds. Women have techniques to win. This is unlike men who see it as a social right, devine right, or sex privilege.

For a woman, it is her sexual power, caring techniques, or mandrake application (use of charm). In other words, most women use means of sexual control, that is, if they find out higher sexual drive as a weakness to the man. Some, it is by fervent affection, mandrake application, or they may take advantage of the man because such a man is deep in love with them. For instance, most women cannot glue in a relationship if they are not in control.

> *For some times in my life, I have had a deep thought on the reason why a woman that God has created to be man's subordinate should rule over man. For example, in majority of marital homes, women are the Acting Head of the families, while men are the Cermonial Heads. However, from the scripture, it is interpreted that a woman's desire shall depend on that of the husband, and the husband shall rule over her.*[36]

---

36. "Unto the woman he said, I will graeatly multiply thy sorrow and thy conception; in sorrow thou shalt bring forth children; and thy desire shall be to thy husband, and he shall rule over thee." See KJV, Genesis 3:16.

The Origin of Control Tussle

> *...that in the beginning there was a gender equality between Adam (the husband) and Eve (the wife), until the wife was cursed due to her offence, thus Adam became in control, or probably Eve was in control of the marriage before their downfall.*

To people of the Christian faith, the origin why women seek control in LR can be track from the teaching of creation in the Bible. I am having some views; first, that in the beginning there was a gender equality between Adam (the husband) and Eve (the wife), until the wife was cursed due to her offence, thus Adam became in control. Secondly, probably Eve was in control of the marriage before their downfall. This is because the instruction of the forbidden fruit was given to Adam when Eve was not yet created. However, she influenced him to eat the fruit, and even Adam confessed it to God[37]. Perhaps you may not accept these views, but I still believed that in the beginning, it is either nobody was in control or the woman was in control before their downfall.

Relatively to our today's experiences, women are still struggling to regain the lost power that took place in the Garden of Eden. But, from the scripture, and societal norms, it is institutionalised that they are to be subordinate to men, despite the global development preaching of gender equality.

Although, that is of biblical viewpoint, in psychological viewpoint, a person may be struggling to be in control of a relationship due to personality influence, such as inferiority complex, perscution complex, superiority complex, or conflict complex, which is a struggle for dominance between ones inferiority and superiority complex.

Now the question remains, who shall be in control? Who to be in control is open for anybody that is in good physical and emotional state to be in control.

Nevertheless, before explaining further, let us get this issue settled. Once we go into relationship, we can be functioning in the thought of our relationship in two different ways, first, through the conscious mind, and second, through the subconscious mind. For instance, some people allow the thoughts of their conscious mind to rule them, while some allow that of the subconscious mind to rule them.

---

37. "And the LORD God commanded the man, saying, Of every tree of the garden thou mayest freely eat: But of the tree of the knowledge of good and evil, thou shalt not eat of it: for in the day that thou eatest thereof thou shalt surely die." See KJV, Genesis 2:16-17. "And the man said, The woman whom thou gavest to be with me, she gave me of the tree, and I did eat." See KJV, Genesis 3:12

From the interpretation of Harry W. Carpenter works:

Most thoughts in the conscious mind are communicated by an inner or outer voice. Most, although not all, thinking uses a voice, and a voice uses words. The conscious mind communicates predominantly with words, and the subconscious mind communicates predominantly with images and feelings.

In cognitive process, our conscious mind is logical. It has the ability to think, think abstractly, reason, criticize, analyze, judge, choose, select, discriminate, plan, invent and compose, use hindsight and foresight. It uses both deductive and inductive reasoning. This is unlike the subconscious mind, conversely, is not logical; it is the feeling mind. It is the source of love hatred, anguish, fear, jealousy, sadness, anger, joy, desire, et cetera. In addition, the conscious mind can stimuate the subconscious mind into action, cause it to change habits, reverse negative thinking patterns, improve our physical and emotional health, often responding to positive thoughts, etc.[38]

From this point, those whom the thought of subconscious mind rules their lives, are the people that always dwell on the particularity of their partners, and they are bound to lack control because they fall in love so deeply. However, those of the conscious dwelling people are bound to control because they are conscious of themselves.

Although, there is a chance for one to be in better control, but it requires a little task. The task is the ability of the person to communicate the *boundaries cum principles* of the relationship from the conscious side of the mind into the subconscious mind, thereby through the conscious mind stimulates the subconscious mind into action, relative to the 'WILL' of the conscious mind. This is where the whole issues reside.

From the question of "who shall be in control", when two people are into a relationship, and establsihed love boundaries cum principles of the relationship, the person to be in control must be the one who has developed a means of effective communication between his or her conscious and subconscious mind. The person must be a person of single-minded or willpower rules-person. So the person must have the ability of making the conscious mind to stimulate the subconscious mind into a positive action, relatively to decisions established in the boundaries cum principles of the relationship. Thus, in eventuality of decision-making, action, or response toward any circumstance that concern the relationship, there may not be a conflict between the conscious and subconscious mind in carrying action, whereby resulting to double-minded or lack of willpower.

---

38. The discussed communication pattern and cognitive process of the conscious and subconscious mind is an interpretation from the work of Harry W. Carpenter in his book titled "The Power of Your Subconscious Mind". See page 37, 38, 40 and 41.

The implication is that those who fall in the above position never allow their feeling of love or particularity of their partner to control their decision, so they are always in control whenever they meet the opposite side. In addition, even if emotion drives them, but it is always the rightful thought type, and they are single-minded persons who live strongly on their willpower.

The opposite side is the persons or people who have ineffective conscious and subconscious mind communication attitude. To such persons, in decision taking, they can be seen as weak people, who lack the power to communicate the *boundaries cum principles* from the conscious mind into the subconscious side. They are in most cases emotional-driven persons due to much dwelling on the imagination of their partner's particularity. For instance, in an eventuality of responding to a particular condition that requires decision-making, relatively to their relationship, the conscious mind through the 'Will' may provide very good decision to be taken, however, the subconscious mind, which is occupied with feeling of love or their partner's particularity may involuntarily take the place of the decision-making through the 'Power' of feeling of love that is being driven by emotion, therefore, cause lack of 'willpower', and emotional rules in the person, due to the conflict between the conscious and subconscious mind in the person[39].

Normally, the affected person will find it hard to control his/her relationship decisions, and once the person fails to control his/her relationship decision, the person cannot as well control his or her existing relationship.

The implication is that this kind of persons are more emotional-driven as a result of the particularity of their partner, and what has realy affected them is that, in their *alpha-state*, they spend more time in thinking, meditating, and imagining the particularity of their loved ones. The only benefit is that they enjoy the ecstacy of the love relationship than their opposite, but they are prone to heartbreak in case of disappointment or breakup.

---

39. Whenever there is a conflict between the subconscious and conscious mind, the subconscious mind, which communicates with image will overpower the conscious mind, which communicates with words. This is why those who dwell much on the particularities of the partners lack willpower.

General point

Generally, the truth is that whatever kind of attitude we displayed, decision taken, or implemented are often emanated from our subconscious mind. Our conscious mind can make both good and bad decisions, but it cannot execute any, if it is in conflict with the subconscious part. Therefore, how we relate in a relationship depends on the information the concious mind can convey to the subconscious mind. For instance, if we convey information corresponding to *characters-control*, then we may be able to be in control relatively to the affected area. Therefore, in every relationship, we are expected to be more emotional to the *boundaries cum principles* of the relationship than the particularity of our partner. For instance, we are emotional to a circumstance only when it is in our subconscious mind. This is because emotion is the power of the subconscious mind, it communicates with image or feeling, and whenever there is a conflict between the '*will*' of the conscious mind, and the '*image (or power)*' of the subconscious mind, the image will often prevail.

Fear and Control Driver

Fear is an unpleasant feeling caused by panic, untrust, danger, et cetera. Most times in our love relationship, we may develop fear of separation, rejection, or cheating, thus get angry, anxious, or unhappy.

In cogent argument, some believed that fear experienced in LR does not come from love, while some argued that fear is a part of risk that we found when being in love. However, fear is not love, and love is not fear, but existing conditions or circumstances in relationship can effect or create an atmospheric fear in LR. Remember the fear of untrust, separation, or rejection, which can emanate when a person into a LR is not feeling terribly good about the LR.

For the major cause of fear, people who failed to develop self-awareness, self-acceptance, and high self-esteem of themselves often feel terribly bad in their LR, thus dwell in fear. By living in fear, their mode of happiness becomes dependent on their partner's decision and behaviour. For instance, if a person feels empty of himself/herself before a partner appears into his/her life, that person may dwell in the fear that the partner should not leave, because if the partner does, the emptiness may return. So the partner becomes paramount, thus remain in control of the LR.

However, to be in control or independent is the ability of the person to create self-awareness, self-acceptance, and high self-esteem of herself/himself within the *boundaries cum principles* of the LR.

How to Dismiss fear in LR

This requires two set of activities, first, the ability to create self-awareness, self-acceptance, and high self-esteem. Secondly, the ability to communicate them into the subconscious mind through the conscious part of the mind.

To develop self-awareness, self-acceptance, and high self-esteem, we can run the following activities:

1.　*State five adjectives that best describe you, for example, I am independent of anybody.*

2.　*Highlight your major goal or dream, for example, I want to be the Govenor of my State.*

3.　*Write down your four strengths, for example, I often keep my words.*

4.　*Write down your four weaknesses, for example I am too defensive.*

5.　*Write down how to improve both your strengths and weaknesses, for example I will not accept any predatory advance, I will always hold my words, etc.*

Now to communicate the created self-awareness, self-acceptance, and high self-esteem into the subconscious mind, follow the activities of abiding with the laws of the subconscious mind. These laws include the law of *Repetition, Emotion, Present Tense, One Dominant Concept, Expectation, Reverse Effect,* and *Resistance.*

Repetition: The created actions of the self-awareness, self-acceptance, and high self-esteem accepted by the subconscious mind must be nurtured. For instance, in programming them into the subconscious mind, it is necessary to repeat them always until they are completely accepted by the subconscious mind. After it is accepted, they should be repeated periodically to ensure that they remain dominant.

Emotion: Attaching emotion to a suggestion makes it more effective. Emotion is the power of the subcoscious mind. For the subconscious mind to be successful in the use of the actions of the self-awareness, self-acceptance, and high self-esteem, they all must be in attachment with emotional state of the mind.

Present Tense: The conscious mind lives by time, namely past, present, and future, whereas the subconsicou mind only lives in the present. In the subconscious mind, the past is merely present recollections and the future is present predictions, therefore the created actions of the self-awareness, self-acceptance, and high self-esteem must be often perceived to be present tense.

One Dominant Concept: The subconscious mind will acccept only one concept to be true at existing anytime. Although, more than one concept (thought, habit, program) can be held in the it (subconscious mind) at the same time, but only one will be binding. Thus, when the subconscious mind recognizes a concept as true, that concept guides and dominates ones actions. So it is good for the person to always dwell and practise the created actions of the self-awareness, self-acceptance, and high self-esteem in order to have them dominate the person's actions.

Expectation: The subconscious mind is like a goal seeking computer. Whatever goal supplied, it seeks to fulfill them. For instance, "a sincere expectation" can be a goal given to your subconscious mind, and the law can be stated, when the subcoscious mind expects something, it makes that thing happen. In this law, the developed actions of the self-awareness, self-acceptance, and high self-esteem must be in expectation.

Behind The Attitude of Been-in-Control

Domineering attitude is a general trait resulting from the personality component of '*id*'. It can be manifesting in those who have *low ego-strength*, and are been ruled by *Sigmund Freud pleasure principle*. Many people have this trait and often feel to be in control or dominate in every LR, and even in other issues, they found themselves.

For self-awareness, there are people who have this trait, they are aware, and exhibit it unconsciously towards people. To most of them, they want to amend it, so that they will not be offending some people, but could not, because the resultant action is involuntarily. In other words, they do not know why they are acting that way. For instance, most women in this behavioural pattern always want to control their opposite partners. But, there are people who have this trait and they are not aware of it, and they subconsciously demonstrate it unwantedly to people. Although, the discussion is not on "who is aware, and who is not aware", but on the driving force behind the trait.

According to Sigmund Freud an Austrian neurologist who created the ideas of id, ego, and super-ego[40]:

> The id: *This is the only component of personality that is present from birth. This aspect of personality is unconscious and includes of the instinctive and primitive behaviors. It is driven by the pleasure principle, which strives for immediate gratification of all desires, wants, and needs. If these needs are not satisfied immediately, the result is a state of anxiety or tension.*
>
> *However, immediate satisfying of these needs is not always realistic or even possible. If we were ruled entirely by the pleasure principle, we might find ourselves grabbing things we want out of other people's hands to satisfy our own cravings. This sort of behavior would be both disruptive and socially unacceptable. The id tries to resolve the tension created by the pleasure principle through the primary process, which involves forming a mental image of the desired object as a way of satisfying the need.*
>
> The ego: *This is the component of personality that is responsible for dealing with reality. The ego develops from the id and ensures that the impulses of the id can be expressed in a manner acceptable in the real world. The ego functions in the conscious, preconscious, and unconscious mind.*

The ego operates based on the reality principle*, which strives to satisfy the id's desires in realistic and socially appropriate ways. The reality principle weighs the costs and benefits of an action before deciding to act upon or abandon impulses. In many cases, the id's impulses can be satisfied through a process of delayed gratification--the ego will eventually allow the behavior, but only in the appropriate time and place.*

The super-ego: *The last component of personality to develop is the super-ego. The super-ego is the aspect of personality that holds all of our internalized moral standards and ideas that we acquire from both parents and society--our sense of right and wrong. The super-ego provides guidelines for making judgments. The super-ego begins to emerge at around age five.*

The Interaction of the Id, Ego and Superego

With so many competing forces, it is easy to see how conflict might arise between the id, ego and super-ego. Freud used the term ego strength *to refer to the ego's ability to function despite these dueling forces. A person with good ego strength is able to effectively manage these pressures, while those with too much or too little ego strength can become too unyielding or too disrupting[40].*

In Freudian psychoanalytic theory that we briefly explained above, the '*id*' is the part of the psyche that is unconscious and the source of primitive instinctive impulses and drives[41]. It is unconscious in nature, thus exists as part of psych in the subconscious side of the mind. It drives us when we lack the ability to control or mask our inferiority or superiority complex. In other words, it is been powered by emotion, and influence on our behaviour, or work as a set of related feelings, ideas, or impulses that may be repressed on us, but continues to influence our thoughts and behaviour relatively to how we want to relate with other people. However, this is solely depends on our *ego strength* to control it. As Freud identified, its manifestation depends on *ego strength* against competing forces that might emanate in the conflict between itself (the id), ego, and super-ego.

40. The Id, Ego and Superego, The Structural Model of Personality, By Kendra Cherry, About.com Guide
http://psychology.about.com/od/theoriesofpersonality/a/personalityelem.htm
41. Microsoft® Encarta® 2009. © 1993-2008 Microsoft Corporation. All rights reserved.

In a likely manner, this is where the concept of conscious and subconscious mind is involved. Therefore, we are not going to argue it, if we say; the 'id' is part of the subconscious mind, and the ego and super-ego are of the conscious mind. Now if the 'id' exists in the subconscious mind, and the ego and super-ego components of personality exist in the conscious mind, there is no doubt over their conflict in terms of need or reponse.

Similarly, an improper communication between the subconscious and conscious part will always result to conflict, thus allowing the subconscious side to prevail. This is similar to-how a low ego-strength will often pave way for the ego to respond according to the need of the 'id'.

Unconscious Domineering Persons

People who unconsciously display the domineering trait in their LR are subjected under the influence of the above expression of 'id', ego, and super-ego relatively to the subconscious and conscious mind, which we just discussed. Their two fundamental problems are first, they lack the ability to communicate their real identity from their conscious mind into their subconscious mind properly. Secondly, they are not yet able to articulate the definition of *"who they are"*, and cannot hold a clear picture of *"who they are"*, in some circumstances, so they suffer low self-esteem or self-exaggeration tendency, thus unconsciously arrogate sense of domineering to themselves in most cases.

However, if you always feel inferior at every relationship confrontation or interaction, know that your subconscious mind is filled up with inferiority thoughts, and these thoughts will always serve as impulse at every interaction, including in a LR. In other hand, if you always feel superior at every relationship interaction, know that your subconscious mind is filled up with superiority thoughts, and these thoughts will always serve as impulse at every interaction, including in a LR. Therefore, a person of inferiority complex in a particular LR is bound to be under the control of the opposite partner despite, how he/she might struggle to overcome the condition. For instance, if the conscious part of the mind is holding the superiority complex by *'will'*, and the subconscious part holds the inferiority complex by *'image'*, in case of confrontation, there will be a conflict between the inferiority and superiority complex, but the inferiority thoughts will prevail.

However, there is exceptional case, where the circumstance will produce an antagonistic result that will forcefully make the person under inferiority complex to impose control on the opposite partner. Although, if the situation appear in this form, understand that the result may be the inferiority person is trying to defend his or her complex.

For superiority, a person filled up with superiority thoughts in the subconscious mind will unconsciously be *in control* over his/her partner in relationship. For instance, if the conscious part of the mind holds the inferiority complex by '*will*', and the subconscious part holds the superiority complex by '*image*', in case of confrontation, there will be a conflict between the inferiority and superiority complex, but the superiority thoughts will prevail.

However, there is exceptional case, where the circumstance will produce an antagonistic result that will forcefully make the person who is under subconscious inferiority complex to impose control on the subconscious superiority complex person. Although, if the situation appear in this form, understand that the result may be due to an external force, which may lead the inferiority person trying to defend his or her complex.

Conscious Rule Persons

In a LR, the conscious rules people control, but do not dominate. They do not have pronounced domineering trait. They know who they are, who is better than them, and whom they are better than. For instance, a conscious rules person has properly communicated his or her principles into the subconscious mind via their conscious mind. The person is aware of his/her personality. He or she lives with *high ego-strength*.

From the work of Freud that aforementioned, people in the above expression are being rule by the *reality principle*. This positions their ego to respond strongly and rightly by absorbing the pressure and tension provided by the 'id' in terms of pressing need, and as well internalised the factors of the super-ego to do the right things almost at the right time. For example, if it is a man, he remains in charge and control of the LR, but, if it is a woman, she will relegate herself to the order of the man.

Nevertheless, to be realistic of what is happening today in the real world, in a LR of two conscious rule persons, the control of the relationship does not reside permanently in one person. For instance, sometimes, the man will be in charge, however in some occasions also, the woman may takeover to be in charge, and this is how the trend moves.

Chapter Four

THE POWER OF MARGINAL UTILITY

Introduction

Man is predisposed as a rule by nature to rise or decline his value, and desire on anything that yeild satisfaction base on the phenemenon of abundancy, and scarcity. In this form of his nature, he assigned a high value to things he struggled to acquire, may be due to scarcity, and despised the things he suffer not much to get, may be due to abundancy.

Just like the classical economists of 20th century argued over human consumption,

> ...water is more important than diamond, but diamond is more valued than water.

The same is applicable in love-relationship (LR), for instance, when we show much love to a loved one, in most cases we get despise, but if we deny the person most of the activities such as *too much caring*, the person will appreciate the little we offered. What actually caused this effect is the power of Marginal Utilty (MU) and Total Utility (TU) relative to the psychological state of man, in terms of satisfaction. It is the power of MU and TU that worked in our pysche, therefore made us to respond and behave in that manner.

The Impact of Marginal Utility in LR

The inclusion of marginal utility (MU) might look like a confuse issue in relation to the previous chapters, but, it has a lot to unfold. For the purpose of comprehensiveness, we must acknowledge the commonest four phenemena we are experiencing in our relationship. They are *desire, value, satisfaction,* and *labour of love.*

Desire: It is the strong feeling of wanting something, perhaps from one's partner or expected person. For example, desire for possession, marriage, sex, caring, to be love, to love, et cetera.

Value: It indicates the level of opinion or appreciation that a person has towards a partner, or expected partner personality, or particularity, including the person's effort to the betterment of a love-relationship (LR). In other words, it signifies how we value our partner, including the person's efforts over the betterment of our relationship. For example, the value we attribute to a person we love or about to love.

Labour of Love: These are those tasks we do in order to make sure that our relationship moves smoothly. We do them for the sake of the relationship. For example, sex indulgence, caring, showing of respect, doing anything morally good to make our partner feels good and remains happy, makng ourselves admirable, et cetera.

Utility: In this context, it is the satisfaction we derived from being in a love relationship. Utility as the case may be in every relationship does not flow constantly. Its existence depends on the outcome of the relationship forces. It exists in the *Nova phase,* and may disappear in the *Sombre,* and *Ebb phases.* Examples of utility we enjoy in our relationship include the satisfaction derived from sexual intercourse with our partner, the person way of showing affections to us, the physical attractiveness of the person, partner's love technique of handling us, et cetera.

How MU and TU Determine our Love Partner

The concept of Marginal Utility (MU), and Total Utility (TU) in this book is to illuminate the strong tendencies that help us to keep our relationship, or select a partner when going into any LR.

In a strict economic term, *MU is an additional satisfaction a consumer can derive from the consumption of an extra unit of a given commodity, given the price of that commodity at a particular point in time.* In other words, relating to a layman view, *it is an additional pleasure or enjoyment a person can enjoy from an additional use of a thing, given the value of that thing (perhaps the price) at a particular point in time.*

For application, the MU of any LR is the additional enjoyment we can derive from remaining in that LR, observing the value of the relationship in a particular period, say three years.

In other way, the MU of sexual indulgence in a relationship is the additional satisfaction, we can derive from having a second chance of sexual activity with our partner, given the value we derive from the first one we had in a particular point in time.

In the other hand, the *TU is the total satisfaction a consumer can derive from the consumption of a given commodity, given the price of the commodity in a particular point of time.* To a layman view, *it is the total pleasure or enjoyment a person can enjoy from the outcome of an existing relationship in a particular point in time.*

Moreover, most economists believed that the decision of a consumer to buy a particular commodity in the varieties of others is depending on the TU of the choosen commodity. So to them, TU is assumed as equal to price, thus to simulate this condition, the *higher the TU of a particular commodity, the higher the demand for the commodity, and the lower the MU of that commodity.*

This is because as the consumer consumes the given commodity continually, the TU of the commodity will increase, but its MU will decrease continually until when the commodity will no longer be able to yeild any additional satisfaction to the consumer. But, the decision to buy an extra unit of that commodity depend on its MU (i.e., the additional satisfaction to gain), as MU is also assumed to be equal to price.

Relatively, the above positions are applicable to us when we are in search of a life partner or loved one for a love relationship. But, before proceeding, let us clear this question. *Is labour of love a commodity?*

Commodity in a strict economic term is the generic term of good and service. A good is anything tangible that can be use to satisfy human wants, e.g. television. In other hand, a service is any intangible thing in form of activity that can also provide satisfaction. These include teaching services we get from our teachers, labour of love service we get from our love partners, et cetera. From this point, logically, commodity stands for good and services, and service is of labour of love in nature, thus labour of love can be use in the same manner commodity is used.

Now, in the continuation of TU, the decision of a person to make choice of a partner, in the varieties of many persons depend on the *anticipated total satisfaction (ex-ante utility)* that person may benefit from the prefered person's labour of love. That is to say, the ability of a man to make choice of a woman, in the varieties of many women is depending on the anticipated total satisfaction the man may enjoy from the woman's labour of love. In addition, the anticipated total satisfaction is assumed to be equal with the total effort the man may put in order to have the woman. Moreover, the same situation is applicable to women, whenever they are to make choice in the varieties of men.

To the MU, the ability of a person to still keep his or her partner, or remain steadfast in an existing relationship depends on the *anticipated additional satisfaction* the person may enjoy by remaining in that relationship or not abandoning the relationship. That is to say, the ability of a man to still keep a woman as his partner or to remain steadfast in his LR with a particular woman depends on the *anticipated additional satisfaction* he may enjoy from the woman's additional labour of love. Take for instance; do you know why most times a man will jilt a woman after sexually satisfying himself from her body?

It is because the *anticipated additional satisfaction* he may enjoy by mating with the woman for the second time or subsquent times is less than the total effort; (including money to be spend), he may put in order to continue mating with the woman[42]. The same is applicable to women when they jilt a man. They often consider the *anticipated additional satisfaction* to gain, assming they remain with the man. Although, it is this phenemenon that bred some comments like;

> *"She does not worth my time, or she is not my kind of person."*

---

42. Remember that indulging into sex with a person is a service offerred, but it is a service in the labour of love, or labour of payment (i.e. in the case of prostitution).

The role of Lust, Attraction, and Attachment

The analysis of how MU and TU can contribute in helping us to make choice of a love partner is in aligned with the products or effect of lust, attraction, and attachment.

The TU and MU enable us to assume the total satisfaction and additional satisfaction respectively, which we may derive in stages of lust, attraction, and attachment of LR, especially as we are to make choice of a partner. For instance, *mating satisfaction from lust, the longevity of the physical attraction of the body of our partner that will result from the attraction, the anticipated achievement of the loved one contribution, and what his or her presences may bring to the our live-that will emanate from attachment.*

However, one may ask, how can the satisfactions or enjoyment resulting from the product of lust, attraction, and attachment be measured?

In strict economic application, *the satisfaction such as TU, MU, derived from the consumption of commodities are measures in utils.* However, the satisfactions we derive from the product of lust, attraction, and attachment are qualitative, and cannot be directly quantified, therefore, we adopt the idea of "assumed-value (AV)" of LR[43].

The Assumed-Values (AV) of LR Satisfaction

The enjoyment or satisfaction we dervied from TU and MU of our loved one labour of love are uncalculated, but, we can measure their assumed-values (AV), which are qualitative and quantitative values derived through assumption of some situational variables. In other words, they are imaginary judgement, discernment, or uncalculated values we derive from the product of lust, attraction, and attachment, or generally, labour of love.

The AV of Lust

As we learnt in chapter two, the first stage of LR is lust, which is the passionate sexual desire that promotes mating between lovers. Some love experts[44] stated that the lust stage often lasts only for few weeks or months, and sometimes depending on the people involved.

In mating experience, there is a satisfaction that flows out. This satisfaction attains to a point of pick, when the two that are matng reach their climax or orgasm. At this point, they derived their total satisfaction of mating with each other.

---

43. I formulated the idea of AV to enable me measure the satisfactions of lust, attraction, and attachment. It is has no specific formula, but for the analyses of satisfaction.

44. Like Winston, Robert (2004). Human. Smithsonian Institution. ISBN 0-03-093780-9 See http://en.wikipedia.org/wiki/Love#cite_note-brain_systems-18.

Moreover, if that is their second time, *all things being equal (ceteris paribus)*, the total satisfaction will be less compare to that of the first time, thus the additional satisfaction of the current mating experience will reduced. If this continues, there will be a point where they will no longer lust for each other except for child bearing purposes, assuming they are married.

So in choosing a life partner, it is necessary to make an assumption of how long both of you can lust for each other. This is where the AV of lust plays part. The longer the period both of you can lust for each other, the better the LR, especially in the case of marriage.

Remember that the AV of lust can last for weeks, and perhaps months depending on the couple's level of lust to each other.

The AV of Attraction

As we also learnt in chapter two, the second stage of LR is attraction, which encourages people to focus on likening each other. Some expert[45] said this stage (attraction) normally lasts from one and a half to three years. Meaning that when searching for a life partner, we should expect an AV of attraction ranging from one and a half to three years or more from the person we decided to choose as a partner. Moreover, one thing to understand is that attraction does not only contain the physical appearance of a loved one, but also the particularity of the person and, most of the particularities exist in attachment form. Although, the AV of attraction such as of physical appearance of the body declines with time. For instance, let us look into this case:

> *A young man of 36 years of age wants to marry a young lady of 29 years of age. He has to consider how the lady may appear or look at the age of say 56-60 years. Assuming the lady's physical appearance will fade around that 56-60 years that he assumed, the* total satisfaction *of the AV of attraction of the lady will be between the range of 27-31 years, and the* additional satisfaction *of the AV of attraction of the lady is after the period of her 56-60 years of age until when she will die. The high the additional satisfaction, which cannot be measure except by assumption, the better the LR, ceteris paribus, vice-versa.*

We should often consider the total and additional satisfaction of the AV of attraction of the person we want to spend our entire life. Although, the quality of physical appearance of people varies, and it depends on nature, hereditary, diet, et cetera.

---

45. Like Winston, Robert (2004). Human. Smithsonian Institution. ISBN 0-03-093780-9 See http://en.wikipedia.org/wiki/Love#cite_note-brain_systems-18.

The AV of Attachment

Attachment is the last stage of LR. As we learnt in chapter two, it is attachment, which can lead LR into marriage. Although no specific period of range is assign to it, but Winston (2004)[46] maintains that it can last for years, perhaps decades. However, most products of attachment are:

- *the expected contribution a loved one can render in order to enable the received-partner achieve his or her ultimate goal or dream in life,*
- *the desired to have a child from a particular partner,*
- *loved one family background,*
- *religious types, and others, classified in value and belief system.*

In a whole, the products of attachment are in the content of particularity of the loved one. Therefore, *the total satisfaction of AV of attachment is the anticipated help for example, a woman has to contribute in order to help his partner achieve his dreams, probable life dream.* The man who received this help can quantify or qualify the satisfaction base on the level of the goals achieved. *The satisfaction to derive after achieving of the ultimate goal is the additional satisfaction of the AV of the attachment.* For example, a man can marry a lady just for the benefit of using her in achieving a particular goal. In this case, *the total satisfaction of the AV of the attachment is the satisfaction the man will enjoy by attaining the goal.* In addition, *the additional satisfaction of the attachment is the satisfaction the man may derive by still keeping the lady, after he has achieved that particular purpose that made him to marry her.* If the additional satisfaction of the AV of the attachment is low, the man may jilt the lady, which is popularly called 'used and dumped' circumstance.

46. Like Winston, Robert (2004). Human. Smithsonian Institution. ISBN 0-03-093780-9
http://en.wikipedia.org/wiki/Love#cite_note-brain_systems-18

The Natural Weakness of Desire, Value, and Satisfaction

Both MU and TU are powerful psychological stimulants in the issues of human behaviour relatively to desire, value, and satisfaction. However, there is this universal weakness working in us relatively to desire, value, and satisfaction. This natural weakness exists due to the psychological response in us toward them. *We are predisposed as a rule by nature to rise or decline our value, and desire on the thing or activities that yeild satisfaction base on the phenemenon of abundancy (plentious availability), and scarcity (less availability).* That is to say, any object, which is easily to be reach or acquired will face less value, thus lesser or no desire at all. But those that are difficult to reach or not even reachable will attract higher value, thus higher desire. In other way, anything we acquired without much effort or higher cost may generally be unappreciated, discredited, or disregard. This is unlike the things we put much effort to get, they will be highly appreciated, regard and desired more.

> *I cannot forget the classical economists' argument of 20th Century in the 'paradox of value', the argument was on the reason why water is more important than diamond, but diamond is more desired, and valued than water. Most economists at that time held a view that the responsible factor is cost of production, while some said it is the TU. However, some economists came with the concept of the MU. To them, the MU of water is easy to attain due to its full availability, and the MU of diamond is difficult to attain when compare to that of water due to its less availability.*[47]

Relatively, the above position is applicable to our relationship. For instance, when our labour of love (e.g. caring) is too much available to our love partner, we may actually be less appreciated, and most cases treat with despise, ceteris paribus. But, this is our nature, and that is how we behave. It is a psychological state, which exists, and works in us as a concept of MU.

---

47. Although there may be someplaces in the world where there is existing shortage of water, but I still believed that, there is no place on this earth where water can be use for exchange of diamond.

How MU Works in the Mindset: A case of hit track of music

Do you remember the first time you heard a particular hit track of a musical album, the feeling and value you developed, and how more you desired to play it, but, as you play it continually, both your initial feeling and desire began to decline until the period when you lost the interest of the track. Though, in most of the time, when you hear the same track again, may be after an interval of time (say some years), you were excited, and desire to play it more and more.

Anyway, what took place in you is of psychological impact within your state of mind, relative to MU as a function of your desire, and value within that period. For instance, at the first time you heard the track, the willingness to play it more was there, you desired to play it more. But, as you play it continually, the total satisfaction (TU) you derived from the track rises, while the additional satisfaction (MU) declines, and as you continually listening to the track, you reached your saturation point where the TU is at its maximum point, which is the point where you are fully satisfied of hearing the track. However, at this point, there was no need of any additional satisfaction or repeatition of the track, so to listen to the track more was no longer interesting you. But, after sometime, due to you have not heard the track again for a longtime, therefore anytime you hear it either some where, you got excited and desires to listen more of it.

From the explanation of the above, what really makes you indifferent of the track is its abundancy, which makes it available for you whenever you are in need to hear it. So as this continues, you attained the indifferent point, where the track no longer interests you. But, by keeping it aside, and staying away from it for long, then you missed it, especially as you hear it some other places.

The foregoing is also the same situation in our relationship. When we make our labour of love too much available by always being present to our partner, we create ourselves to be taking for granted.

> What I mean by our labour of love to be too much available are; doing almost everything possible to make our relationship works smoothly, whether those things are pleasing us or not. These include sexual indulgence, excessive showing of caring, respect, and tolerance, much defensive for peace to reign, et cetera. For instance, by making your labour of love too much available, the total and additional satisfaction your partner enjoys from your presence will continue to rise. As time goes, since human beings have saturation point in everything they do that give satisfaction, your partner will be tired of the most activities of your labour of love. Once the person is at this point, the person will be reciprocating in the style of contempt or despise. The truth is that, at this point, the person will be indifferent of the additional satisfaction (MU) he/she will derive or enjoy from your labour of love. For example, if it is sexual indulgence, the person may no longer desire you much.

The upshot through experience may have caused you the followings:

- *Why you lost your pride in your relationship,*
- *Why your partner jilted you,*
- *Why your effort is no longer appreciated in your relationship,*
- *Why your partner suddenly cut his or her mutual response,*
- *And others,*

Nevertheless, if you are experiencing any of the above outlined or others, the trial solution is to create artificial scarcity of your labour of love, or withdraw most of them, perhaps disappear (if it is possible).

By doing this, the absent of your labour of love will simulate some actions within the mindset of the person, thus leading the person to desire any of your labour of love. Following the missing of you (or any part of your labour of love), the person's conscious mind may stimulate his or her subconscious mind into action, thereby cause it to change habits, reverse negative, or respond positively to you.[48]

---

48. The analysis of the above is attainable, if only the person loves your particularity. Person, who is not move by your personality, may not care even when you disappear for a long time.

The Law 16 of 48 Laws of Power

From the upshot, Robert Greene in his work titled *"The Conscise: 48 Laws of Power"* observed human beings to possess the nature that we have explained above. So in his work[49], he put it this way:

> *Too much circulation makes the price go down: the more you are seen and heard from, the more common you appear. If you are already established in a group, temporary withdrawal from it will make you more talked about, even more admired. You must learn when to leave. Create value through scarcity.*

He continues,

> *The truth of this law can most easily be appreciated in matters of love and seduction. In the beginning stages of an affair, the lover's absence stimulates your imagination, forming a sort of aura around him or her. But, this aura fades when you know too much - when your imagination no longer has room to roam. The loved one becomes a person like anyone else, a person whose presence is taken for granted.*
>
> *To prevent this, you need to starve the other person of your presence. Force their respect by threatening them with the possiblity that they will lose you for good.*

49.The Concise edition published in Great Britain in 2002 by Profile Books Ltd.

King Solomon's wise sayings of material things and acquisitions

He that loveth silver shall not be satisfied with silver, nor he that loveth abundance with increase: this is also vanity. Ecc. 5:10

From the Scripture, the famous wisest man named; King Solomon, the son of King David of Isreal experienced the effect of MU on availability of material things, including sexual indulgence, and other labour of love, and never hesitate to call them (both his wealth, wives, and concubines) vanity upon vanity.

Properly, something is vanity, when it becomes futile. Whatever that is futile, is of worthless or empty of significance, and whatever that is of empty of significance is less important and less yeilding of satisfaction.

King Solomon in his acquisition of material things including woman, felt them to be vanity because he attained the maximum satisfaction (TU) of them. He was able to called his acquisitions *vanity upon vanity* because he was in the position of not wanting or lacking any of them. He has them at his disposal, thus the additional satisfaction (MU) he enjoys by making use of them while on earth is no longer there. This is because he has attained their total satisfaction (TU), and reaches at their satuaration point as acquired wealth.

However, today, many Christians are lacking the understanding of this point. They are seeing Solomon's wise sayings of material things and their acquisitions as God's instruction to humankind to avoid material acquisitions[50]. This is not true. Solomon saying is of psychological issues relative to all we have explained concerning MU and TU. To him, there is abundancy, and that is the reason, he called them vanity upon vanity after the whole enjoyment.

For benefits, the essense of the foregoing is still the same, which is to fortify our points relatively to LR. Like we mentioned earlier, when we make our labour of love too much available by always been present to our partner, we create ourselves to be taken granted. This is an axiomatic state of the psychological life of man relative to MU and TU.

---

50. God did not forbade us from Wealth Acquisition, like He said "And thou say in thine heart, my power and the might of mine hand hath gotten me this wealth. But thou shalt remember the LORD thy God: for it is He that giveth thee power to get wealth that he may establish his covenant which he swear unto thy fathers, as it is this day. (Deu 8:17-18)."

References/List of Footnotes

1. Bonny Albo of About.Com Guide
(www.dating.about.com/od/intimacy/qt/whatislove.htm)

2. Paul Gray, Hannah Bloch, and Sally Donnelly of Time Inc., 2011,
(www.time.com/time/magazine/article/0,9171,97763,00.html)

3. Alexander Moseley observation is culled from;
www.classical-formations.com. Mind you, that website contents are
bound for updating, sorry if the information is removed or updated
from its present place.

4. The saying over here is attributes to Alexander Moseley, although
he may not be the original writer (which I am not sure), but it was
extracted from a work he did, captioned; *the nature of Love: Eros,
Philia, and Agape*. You google this out with statement "the nature of
love."

5. Mind you that the foregoing topic: *"Nature of Love"* is a quoted work
of Alexander Moseley. You can see footnote 3 and 4 for
information about him.

6. "The Brain" is quoted from the book; "The Power of Your
Subconscious Mind". (Harry W. Carpenter, 2005, pg 33-44)"

7. "The State of Mind" is quoted from the book;"The Power of Your
Subconscious Mind" . (Harry W. Carpenter, 2005, pg 22-24)".

8. Helen Fisher is an expert in the topic of love, in one of her work;
she divided love into three stages, which are lust, attraction, and
attachment. See the link below:
http://en.wikipedia.org/wiki/Helen_Fisher_%28anthropologist%29

9. "The Law of Subconscious Mind" is quoted from the book;
"The Power of Your Subconscious Mind"
(Harry W. Carpenter, 2005, pg 79-95)"

10. That is my position about the definition of love.

11. I coined these Words of Wisdom from that of Napolean Hill, 1963.

12. By Ningthoujam Sandhyarani on (http://www.buzzle.com/articles/causes-of-infatuation.html). Last updated January 22, 2013.

13. Harry Croft is the Medical Director, (Psychyiatrist) of Healthy Place. See www.healthyplace.com, Last update on June 1, 2009.

14. Deuteronomy 5:9

15. See Microsoft® Encarta® 2009. © 1993-2008 Microsoft Corporation. All rights reserved.

16. Like that of the Microsoft® Encarta® 2009. © 1993-2008 Microsoft Corporation.

17. I derived the expression from the economic term of market forces; which is an interaction between demand and supply. In other words, it is a derivative of economic market forces.

18. Aura is a paranormal force emanating from somebody or something: a force that is said to surround all people and objects, discernible, often as a bright glow, only to people of unusual psychic sensitivity. (Microsoft® Encarta® 2009. © 1993-2008 Microsoft Corporation. All rights reserved.)

19. Change in RR stability due to change in situations in which the RR is existing.

20. The observation is only by exprience, and without any scientific research.

21 So I ask, you do not like a person, why given a chance. This is a risk worth not taking. Always adopt Refusal Skill, and not Negotiation Skill.

22. It is quoted from page 43 of the book; "The Power of Your Subconscious Mind" written by Harry W. Carpenter.

23. I personally developed this concept, and its pronounciation is framed from 3Rs (RRR)-FLUCT.

.

24. Although, I have not come across such in any article or book.

25. By parasite, I am referring to a person whose economic sustenance depends on another person's provision. And provider; a person that to cater for the parasite.

26. The functional relationship between a LR and its depending factors, such as an act of material provision.

27. That was during my university undergraduate days.

28. I coined the terms; dog, sheep, and fox base on the behaviour of their relative animals.

29. For those who believed in such spirit.

30. I noticed that there are three phases in a love relationship (especially that of marriage), which permenantly repeat in a circular manner within a period of time. Personally I termed these phases as Nova, Sombre, and Ebb.

31. Heraclitus of Ephesus (ca. 535 – 475 BC) was a pre-Socratic Greek philosopher, a native of Ephesus, Ionia, on the coast of Asia Minor. He is famous for his doctrine of change being central to the universe. His famous sayings, "All is flux", and "You cannot step twice into the same river" is still remembered today.

32. See http://simple.wikipedia.org/wiki/Love

33. See Helen Fisher (2004). Why We Love: The Nature and Chemistry of Romantic love. New York. Henry Holt and Company.

34.   Winston, Robert (2004). Human. Smithsonian Institution.
      ISBN 0-03-093780-9

35.   Remember that indulging into sex with a person is a service, but
      service in the labour of love or labour of payment (as in the case of
      prostitution).

36.   "Unto the woman he said, I will graeatly multiply thy sorrow and
      thy conception; in sorrow thou shalt bring forth children; and thy
      desire shall be to thy husband, and he shall rule over thee." See
      KJV, Genesis 3:16.

37.   "And the LORD God commanded the man, saying, Of every tree
      of the garden thou mayest freely eat: But of the tree of the
      knowledge of good and evil, thou shalt not eat of it: for in the day
      that thou eatest thereof thou shalt surely die." See KJV, Genesis
      2:16-17. "And the man said, The woman whom thou gavest to be
      with me, she gave me of the tree, and I did eat."
      See KJV, Genesis 3:12.

38.   The discussed communication pattern and cognitive process of the
      conscious and subconscious mind is an interpretation from the
      work of Harry W. Carpenter in his book titled "The Power of Your
      Subconscious Mind". See page 37,38, 40 and 41.

39.   Whenever there is a conflict between the subconscious and
      conscious mind, the subconscious mind, which communicates with
      image will overpower the conscious mind, which communicates
      with words. This is why those who dwell much on the
      particularities of the partners lack willpower.

40.   The Id, Ego and Superego,
      The Structural Model of Personality,
      By Kendra Cherry, About.com Guide
      http://psychology.about.com/od/theoriesofpersonality/a/personalityelem.htm

41.   Microsoft® Encarta® 2009. © 1993-2008 Microsoft Corporation.
      All rights reserved.

42.   Remember that indulging into sex with a person is a service offer, but it is a service in the labour of love, or labour of payment (i.e. in the case of prostitution).

43   I formulated the idea of AV to enable me measure on the satisfaction of lust, attraction, and attachment. It is has no specific formula, since, it can be use both in qualitative and quantitative analyses of satisfaction relatively to lust, attraction and attachment.

44.   Like Winston, Robert (2004). Human. Smithsonian Institution. ISBN 0-03-093780-9
      See http://en.wikipedia.org/wiki/Love#cite_note-brain_systems-18

45.   Like Winston, Robert (2004). Human. Smithsonian Institution. ISBN 0-03-093780-9
      See http://en.wikipedia.org/wiki/Love#cite_note-brain_systems-18

46.   Like Winston, Robert (2004). Human. Smithsonian Institution. ISBN 0-03-093780-9
      http://en.wikipedia.org/wiki/Love#cite_note-brain_systems-18

47.   Although there may be some places in the world where there is existing shortage of water, but I still believed there is no place on this earth where water can be use for exchange of diamond.

48.   The analysis of the above is attainable, if only the person loves your particularity. Person, who is not move by your personality, may not care even when you disappear for a long time.

49.   The Concise edition published in Great Britain in 2002 by Profile Books Ltd.

50.   God did not forbade us from Wealth Acquisition, like He said "And thou say in thine heart, my power and the might of mine hand hath gotten me this wealth. But thou shalt remember the LORD thy God: for it is He that giveth thee power to get wealth that he may establish his covenant which he swear unto thy fathers, as it is this day. (Deu 8:17-18)."

Public Review Right

This is to inform you that the author of this book, N. Stephen is willing to welcome public review of this book, therefore you can review the book and send your comment to **spaceeradataservices@hotmail.com**. Alternatively, you can post your comment on **www.onlineworkdata.com/forums**. In addition, questions like "how to contact the author and counseling base on the teachings of this book" is open on the same website link or through the above email address.

Now that you are true with the book, can you answer these questions:

1) What is love? Is it real or ideal?
2) Is there any correlation between romantic relationship and human productivity?
3) Can we differentiate infatuation from love?
4) Is true love attainable?
5) What are the causes of lovesick or lovelorn?
6) Like many people believed, a man loves once in life time", is that true?
7) Is there anyway, we can protect our mind in love relationship?
8) Can I be in control of my relationship?
9) What is my personality type, in love relationship?
10) How do I know reasons why someone accepted me for a relationship?
11) What is behind my unstableness in relationship decision making?
12) I do everything to make him or her happy, yet he never likes them, why?
13) Why do people I love, do not return the same to me?
14) Why in most relationship, we fight for dominance,
15) Please list the boundaries of your LR.

August 2013,

Space-Era Data Services,
of Work Data Group,
www.onlineworkdata.com